W9-ACR-066

PRESIDENT'S COMMISSION
FOR A NATIONAL AGENDA FOR THE EIGHTIES

REPORT OF THE PANEL ON
GOVERNMENT AND THE ADVANCEMENT OF SOCIAL JUSTICE
HEALTH, WELFARE, EDUCATION, AND CIVIL RIGHTS

GOVERNMENT AND
THE ADVANCEMENT OF

Social
Justice

HEALTH, WELFARE, EDUCATION,
AND CIVIL RIGHTS IN THE

Eighties

PRENTICE-HALL, INC., Englewood Cliffs, New Jersey 07632

A SPECTRUM BOOK

This document was prepared by the Panel on Government
and the Advancement of Social Justice: Health, Welfare,
Education, and Civil Rights, one of nine Panels of the
President's Commission for a National Agenda for the
Eighties. The report represents the views of a majority of
the members of the Panel on each point considered. Not
every member of the Panel, including the Chairperson,
agrees with or supports every view or recommendation in
the report. This report was prepared by members of the
Panel without involvement by members of the Commission who were not members of the Panel. This project was
supported by the U.S. Department of Health and Human
Services under provisions of Executive Order 12168, dated
October 24, 1979. Points of view or opinions expressed in
this volume are those of the Panel on Government and the
Advancement of Social Justice, and do not necessarily
represent the official position of the Department.

Library of Congress Cataloging in Publication Data

United States. Panel on Government and the Advance-
    ment of Social Justice: Health, Welfare, Educa-
    tion, and Civil Rights.
    Government and the advancement of social justice.

    (A Spectrum book)
    At head of title: President's Commission for a
National Agenda for the Eighties.
    Reprint. Originally published: Washington :
President's Commission for a National Agenda for the
Eighties, 1980.
    Includes index.
    1. United States—Social policy—1980-
2. Social justice.   I. United States. President's
Commission for a National Agenda for the Eighties.
II. Title.
HN59.2.U54   1981   361.6'1'0973   81-10562
                                            AACR2
ISBN 0-13-360719-4
ISBN 0-13-360701-1 (PBK)

Foreword

As America enters the eighties, our nation faces a world greatly changed from that of even a decade ago. Vast forces are in action at home and abroad that promise to change the lives of all Americans. Some of these forces—such as revolutionary developments in science and technology—hold out hope for longer life, labor-saving mechanisms, exploration of the universe, and other benefits for all peoples. Other forces—such as the growing demand for strategic raw materials under the control of supplier cartels—raise serious problems for all nations. At home, we face serious and unresolved issues in the social and economic structure of American society.

On October 24, 1979, President Jimmy Carter established the President's Commission for a National Agenda for the Eighties. His purpose was to provide the President-elect and the new Congress with the views of 45 Americans drawn from diverse backgrounds outside of government. The group is bipartisan, representing business and labor, science and the humanities, arts and communication. Members of the Commission are experts in many fields, but possess no special expertise in predicting the future. Rather, we have done our best to uncover the dynamics of American society and world affairs that we believe will determine events in the eighties. This report of the Commission, *A National Agenda for the Eighties,* sets forth our views.

The analytical work of the Commission was accomplished by 9 Panels, each consisting of 5 to 11 Commissioners with appropriate staff. The Panels probed into major subject areas designated by the President in the Executive Order that created the Commission, as well as other areas that the Commission itself determined should be on the agenda. This approach gave Panel members an opportunity to gain considerable familiarity with complex subject matters, and provided the full Commission with a wide range of information not otherwise attainable in the 13 months available for this study.

The Panels are responsible for their own reports, and the views contained in any Panel report do not necessarily reflect the views of any branch of government or of the Commission as a whole.

William J. McGill/Chairman
La Jolla, California/December 31, 1980

PRESIDENT'S COMMISSION FOR A NATIONAL

Agenda

FOR THE

Eighties

Chairman
William J. McGill

Daniel Bell	Ruth J. Hinerfeld	Frank Pace, Jr.
Robert S. Benson	Carl Holman	Edmund D. Pellegrino
Charles E. Bishop	Benjamin L. Hooks	Donald C. Platten
Gwendolyn Brooks	Matina S. Horner	Tomás Rivera
J. Fred Bucy, Jr.	Thomas C. Jorling	Paul G. Rogers
Pastora San Juan Cafferty	Rhoda H. Karpatkin	Elspeth D. Rostow
Joan Ganz Cooney	Lane Kirkland	Howard J. Samuels
Marian Wright Edelman	Juanita M. Kreps	Henry B. Schacht
Herman E. Gallegos	Esther Landa	William W. Scranton
John W. Gardner	Theodore R. Marmor	Lewis Thomas
Don L. Gevirtz	Martin E. Marty	Foy Valentine
C. Jackson Grayson, Jr.	Michael McCloskey	Glenn E. Watts
Philip Handler	William E. Miller	Marina v. N. Whitman
Dorothy I. Height	Alan B. Morrison	Addie L. Wyatt
William A. Hewitt	Roger G. Noll	

Co-Staff Directors
Claude E. Barfield   Richard A. Wegman

Preface

The report of the Panel on the Government and the Advancement of Social Justice reflects the collective judgment of nine Commissioners who believe that social justice is a matter of vital concern to this nation. Although we do not agree on every detail, the Commissioners feel that the areas of civil rights, health, welfare, education, and criminal justice, and the specific proposals contained here, deserve serious consideration during the 1980s.

In writing this report, we have attempted to highlight the items that we feel should take priority; we have also tried to make hard choices and be selective about what is included in the report. We have met on a number of occasions to refine our thinking and to listen to expert testimony concerning the subjects covered here.

There is no doubt that past struggles for social justice have left several uncompleted agendas. These agendas include equal rights for all, adequate health care, the guarantee of a minimum income, a quality, desegregated education system, and a fair and humane system of criminal justice.

We call on the President and the Congress to help make social justice a reality in this decade. In pursuit of this goal, we submit this Panel report.

We express special thanks to the organizations that served as our hosts for outreach activities across the country: the National Association for the Advancement of Colored People; the Kennedy Library in Boston, Massachusetts; the University of California at Los Angeles; DePaul University in Chicago; and the Lyndon Baines Johnson Library in Austin, Texas. We would also like to thank the dedicated and hard-working Commission staff who provided valuable assistance.

In particular, we wish to thank Edward D. Berkowitz, who corrdinated the writing of the report and drafted the chapter on welfare. Mary C. Cadette edited the manu script. William L. Jordan took time from his work for the Panel on Government and the Regulation of Corporate and Individual Decisions to help with drafting the criminal justice section. Raymond F. Reisler undertook the difficult task of summarizing and reporting on trends in education. Stuart O. Schweitzer served as our expert on health policy and drafted the health section of this report.

Benjamin L. Hooks
Panel Chairperson

New York, New York
December 31, 1980

GOVERNMENT AND
THE ADVANCEMENT OF

Social Justice

HEALTH, WELFARE, EDUCATION,
AND CIVIL RIGHTS

Chairperson
Benjamin L. Hooks
Executive Director, NAACP

TABLE OF
Contents

Introduction

After studying the nation's problems in the fields of civil rights, health, welfare, education, and criminal justice, the Panel concludes that the nation must improve the existing set of social programs while it continues to pursue these vital social justice goals:

- ☐ An effective guarantee of racial, ethnic, and sexual equality;
- ☐ A health system that will provide all Americans with comprehensive health care produced efficiently at reasonable cost;
- ☐ A welfare system that supplies benefits that guarantee a minimum income;
- ☐ An education system that is accessible to all and that gives all students the chance to develop their talents to the full; and
- ☐ A system of criminal justice that treats all within it fairly and humanely and also deters and controls crime.

The federal government's presence in each of these fields need not be debated; that question was resolved by the passage of the Great Society legislation, including the Elementary and Secondary Education Act of 1964, the Civil Rights Act of 1964, and the Social Security Amendments of 1965 that created Medicare and Medicaid.

Public attention should now be focused on the design and implementation of social programs. The Panel finds that the policymaking process often prevents programs from achieving their ends—for example, programs are sometimes created without sufficient appropriations to support them. In some instances the executive branch fails to follow legislation with a set of consistent regulations to guide program implementation. Nor does promptness in promulgating regulations ensure that programs will meet their goals.

Shortcomings in the policy process are also the result of viewing each program as a separate entity, unrelated to other similar programs. Because of this tendency, the federal government's grant-in-aid programs to further social justice are often fragmented and narrow in scope. At the local level, this fragmentation can lead to inefficiency— administrators are restricted in their ability to initiate new projects and to respond to specific needs.

Another political habit consists of piling program upon program without regard to the system that is being created. This is most apparent in the nation's welfare system, which is an historical catalogue of programs that often work at cross-purposes; for example, programs that seek to help mothers find work are attached to programs that are designed to keep mothers at home with their children. The result is that available money is not spent in a wise manner.

Poorly designed and implemented programs discredit the social objective as much as the particular program involved. The poor suffer from the inadequacies of programs over which they have no control. Society's disappointment with the schools causes hardships for the present generation of students, and public frustration with federal medical insurance programs stifles more fundamental reform of the health care system.

National leadership is required to improve the nation's social programs. There must be creative initiative to improve the health, welfare, and criminal justice systems; the social will and community collaboration necessary to improve the nation's schools; and a strong national commitment to bring about racial and sexual equality.

Even with the best of leadership, the fact that limited resources create hard choices cannot be denied. Hard choices become easier when there is a clear commitment to social goals. The Panel cautions against the desire to dismiss social programs on the grounds that they have failed or that improvements in conditions have rendered them unnecessary. Instead, the country must apply the lessons of the past 20 years to a new generation of social programs and work to cure the conditions that mandate such programs.

There is no question of abandoning the nation's quest for social justice; there is only the necessity to do better. With this spirit the Panel offers a specific agenda to deal with pressing problems in the areas of civil rights, health, welfare, education, and criminal justice.

Civil Rights

The great burst of legislative activity in the 1960s that led to the passage of the Civil Rights Act of 1964, the Voting Rights Act of 1965, and the Fair Housing Amendments of 1968 did not in itself create equality of opportunity. Despite the existence of these laws and the progress that has been made in the past two decades, minority groups

2

and families headed by women do not enjoy equality with the majority. Wide disparities remain in employment and income levels and in gaining access to equal housing and education.

To eradicate these differences, the Panel makes specific recommendations concerning employment training and amending the Fair Housing Act. This Act should provide strong, meaningful enforcement powers to assure minorities, women, and the handicapped of fair housing. In addition, the Panel examines voting rights and concludes that the special protection for minorities in the Voting Rights Act should be extended beyond its present termination date of 1982.

The Panel takes a special look at civil rights issues that affect women and Hispanics. The Panel endorses the concept of equal pay for work of comparable value; it also urges the enactment of the Equal Rights Amendment. Hispanics suffer from the country's inability to sustain a clear policy on the rights of immigrants and from ambivalence over the rights of non-English-speaking citizens. These matters should first be defined and then addressed in a consistent manner.

Health

The nation's health policy also owes a great deal to the Great Society. After 20 years of discussion, Congress passed two federal health insurance programs in 1965. Medicare provided federally funded health insurance for most of the nation's elderly, and Medicaid served as health insurance for many of the nation's poor.

The question of whether the federal government should play a role in health care financing distracted public attention from the differences between the two new programs and the gaps in health insurance that the programs left unfilled. Only the idea of reimbursing local health providers with federal money united the two programs. Despite this injection of federal money into the health system, and despite the extraordinary growth in employer financed health care programs, many Americans remained without health insurance.

One effect of these programs has been to raise the price of medical care to a point at which it is one of the most inflationary items in the national budget. Physicians are customarily reimbursed, not by the consumer, but by a third party such as the federal government or a private insurance company. These third parties can in turn pass along their costs to taxpayers or to individual subscribers. This system provides little incentive for anyone—doctors, insurers, or patients—to control costs.

This Panel recommends a health insurance system that remedies the gaps in coverage and creates incentives for

3

cost containment. In such a system the federal government would give individual families the means to purchase health insurance; families could exercise their own preferences in choosing a health care plan that meets their needs. Such a system may induce health providers to supply care in a more effective manner than is done at present.

The Panel's recommendations extend beyond the financing of health care. The Panel also urges the country to make greater use of preventive medicine; it is more humane, more effective, and less costly to prevent illnesses than to treat their debilitating effects. The nation should make more use of existing technology in this area. It must also give serious consideration to the manner in which it cares for the elderly. Care at home is often preferable to treatment in an institution.

Welfare

The nation's many welfare programs do not provide for all of the poor, nor do they pay adequate benefits to welfare recipients. To remedy the many problems that the programs create or that they fail to solve, the Panel recommends making income maintenance a federal function and creating a minimum security income. This income would be pegged at a level related to the poverty line and would allow recipients to keep a significant portion of their earnings. In this manner adequate benefits would be coupled with incentives for welfare recipients to work. The new program would not make family separation a condition for receiving welfare nor would it permit the wide variation in benefit levels that now occurs from state to state.

Education

Although income maintenance should become a federal responsibility, education should remain a local concern, a vital service that is supplied by communities across the nation. The Panel feels strongly that the public school system, despite its many critics, deserves the nation's support.

The Panel therefore proposes a comprehensive educational agenda based upon the themes of equality, competence, and excellence. The Panel recommends active federal support for activities that lead to a quality integrated education and the desegregation of the nation's schools, such as redistricting, pairing of schools, and court-approved transportation plans. In addition, the Panel believes that support for bilingual, pre-elementary, and remedial education and for education for the handicapped is required to promote equality.

At the elementary school level, there is a need to make a renewed commitment to basic skills so that all students may achieve competence in reading, writing, and arithmetic reasoning. Minimum levels of competence, however, should not be substituted for excellence: schools also have an obligation to maximize the talents of all their students.

In the pursuit of excellence, schools may wish to consider a number of innovative proposals. Although school philosophy and structure emphasize the primacy of learning in self-contained settings such as the classroom, more real-world experience may be necessary to prepare young people for citizenship and family responsibilities. Finally, consideration should be given to restructuring the educational system.

The public schools must put their finances on a firmer footing in order to reach the goals of equality, competence, and excellence. Adequate financial support does not by itself ensure quality education, but helping poorer school districts provide better services is essential to the advancement of social justice. All states should, therefore, seek to reform their school finance systems. Equitable financing of elementary and secondary education, particularly in urban areas, should be regarded by federal and state governments as an integral part of the larger problem of intergovernmental finance for which solutions must be found.

The Panel makes other recommendations that deal with the future of higher education. Through all of these recommendations runs the need for strong leadership in the educational field, leadership that will keep in the public mind a belief that has unified this country in the past: effective education of all children is a public good.

Criminal Justice

This country's criminal justice system should also be fundamentally changed. Each year this system touches in some way one out of four Americans, and experts agree that the crime rate will increase in the 1980s. The Panel finds that improvements can be made in all portions of this large system. The rights of victims must be made a concern. The activities of law enforcement agencies should be monitored so that all citizens receive protection and fair treatment. The bail system and the condition of the nation's jails demand reform. Likewise, the condition of prisons and the range of sentencing options require rethinking and improvement.

These five areas—civil rights, health, welfare, education, and criminal justice—are the major subjects of the report that follows. Not every aspect of these areas receives mention, but the Panel has listed its chief concerns, analyzed the major problems, and proposed measures to solve those problems. Social justice, the Panel concludes, is a subject about which this nation cannot afford to become complacent.

Chapter 1

Civil Rights
AGENDA FOR
THE 1980s

Recent trends in government, the private sector, and public opinion make it essential that the nation's commitment to civil rights be reaffirmed and continued. The 1970s witnessed slippage from the substantial gains of the 1960s, slowing and in some cases reversing the progress made in the elimination of the legacies of past discrimination.

Double-digit inflation, foreign events, problems of energy supply, and other concerns have attracted more and more time of the executive branch and of an increasingly conservative Congress. This has been to the detriment of the concerns of blacks, Hispanics, women, and other disadvantaged groups.

Indeed, several current trends are disturbing. There is even a threat in some recent legislation and litigation that previous civil rights gains may be eroded. Examples include the decision of the 96th Congress not to provide an effective procedure to enforce the Fair Housing Act of 1968, the continuing passage of amendments in Congress directed at preventing federal agencies from enforcing Title VI of the Civil Rights Act of 1964, and the weakening of affirmative action by judicial decisions. There have been court challenges to affirmative action plans in education and employment, and challenges to minority setaside programs for government contracts. Conservative forces have won a judicial battle that will dilute the black vote in majority white voting districts, while judicial and legislative attempts to undermine civil rights are increasing.

Finally, it is neither accidental nor coincidental that the Ku Klux Klan has entered a period of resurgence. The Klan came into being during Reconstruction, and its activities helped to create a climate in which judicial decisions that substantially weakened the rights guaranteed under the 14th and 15th Amendments were considered acceptable.[1]

The current activities of the Klan and other terrorist groups and the growing acceptance by a substantial section of the public of their tactics raise a serious issue. The President and his successors should oppose violence and threats directed against members of minority groups and must reassure them that the full weight of the federal government will be used to protect their rights. Congress should fill those gaps in the federal law that permit racist terror to escape federal prosecution.

The prospect for further progress in civil rights in the 1980s is disturbing. There must be strong Presidential leadership that will create a national climate in which civil rights issues are again addressed with seriousness and intensity. The executive branch must encourage and reward those who implement voluntary affirmative action plans in education and employment opportunities. The executive branch must likewise offer incentives for the development of low and moderate income housing and attack those policies and practices that allow race, color, national origin, religion, sex, or age to determine access to affordable housing in any of this nation's communities.

The executive branch must denounce practices that have the effect of excluding persons because of their race, color, religion, national origin, sex, age, or mental or physical handicap regardless of the intent. The Panel urges that the 1980s be the decade in which the gap between the rhetoric of American promise and the reality of American performance closes.

Background

No country has embraced more wholeheartedly the democratic ideal of equality and, at the same time, experienced greater conflict between this ideal and reality than the United States. Racially discriminatory practices are woven into the social fabric of America.

Since blacks were first brought to this country as slaves, their status has been inferior to that of whites. That status has been explicitly and implicitly sanctioned by the state and federal governments.

Chief Justice Taney, in *Dred Scott* v. *Sanford,* described the legal position of black people in America prior to the Civil War as that of "non-beings."[2] Although the legal status of blacks changed with the adoption of the Civil War Amendments and the passage of the Reconstruction Acts, blacks remained inferior beings in the eyes of the majority.

The 13th Amendment to the Constitution outlawed slavery, but a new system of oppression emerged after the Civil War. Many blacks continued to work the land as tenants of their former masters. In the place of legal slavery came a pernicious system of dependence based on credit. White merchants gave these farmers credit against their crops, usually in the form of tools and agricultural supplies. The system left many blacks in debt, unable to migrate to different areas. Between the Civil War and World War I the majority of blacks continued to live in the South, and their lives sometimes were only legally different from those of slaves.

The Civil Rights Act of 1864 was enacted to aid the enforcement of the 13th Amendment. The Act provided that blacks born in the United States were citizens and, as such, were entitled to the same contract rights as were white persons.

In 1868 the 14th Amendment was ratified to ensure the protection of blacks from state restrictions on liberty based on race, and in 1870 the 15th Amendment guaranteed that the right of blacks to vote would not be infringed by the states. The Civil Rights Act of 1871 implemented the 14th Amendment by providing a direct remedy through federal courts.

The Civil Rights Act of 1871 was followed by the Civil Rights Act of 1875, which provided that no person should be denied the full and equal enjoyment of public facilities because of race or previous condition of servitude. Twenty-one years later, however, the Supreme Court offered the states a legal means of evading the restrictions of the 14th Amendment and the 1875 Act. On July 10, 1890, the Louisiana legislature passed a law to "promote the comfort of passengers" on railroads by providing "separate but equal" accommodations for white and colored passengers. The 1896 case of *Plessy* v. *Ferguson* tested this law;[3] in its decision, the Court interpreted the 14th Amendment as follows:

> The object of the amendment was undoubtedly to enforce the absolute equality of the two races before the law, but in the nature of things it could not have been intended to abolish distinctions based upon color, or to enforce social, as distinguished from political equality, or a commingling of the two races.

The decision in *Plessy* rested on the fallacy that there could be "separate but equal" treatment of people. By the turn of the century, "separate but unequal" had become the rule for black Americans. Enforced segregation, embodied in "Jim Crow" laws, persisted for nearly 60 years in public accommodations, housing, education, employment, and voting. Finally, in 1954, in the landmark case of *Brown* v. *Board of Education,* the Supreme Court concluded that "in the field of education, the doctrine of 'separate but equal' has no place."[4] The Court's decision had a tremendous impact on the struggle of black Americans to achieve equal treatment. Overriding *Plessy,* the *Brown* decision paved the way for successful challenges to the "separate but equal" doctrine in other areas.

By the time of the *Brown* decision, the modern struggle for civil rights was under way. In the 1950s, efforts centered on the repeal of "Jim Crow" laws in the South. The major victories came in the courtroom, but there was also a legislative victory: Congress passed the first civil rights act since Reconstruction in 1957. Intended to counter the stubborn resistance to full voter participation by blacks, the Act created the U.S. Commission on Civil Rights and the Civil Rights Division of the Department of Justice. It also vested the Department of Justice with authority to sue on behalf of blacks denied the right to vote.

In the 1950s and 1960s, civil rights leaders and supporters marched, sat-in, and went to jail in an effort to attain simple justice. Under the leadership of Presidents Kennedy and Johnson, the executive branch took a position in the vanguard of the struggle to end racial discrimination.

Ten years after *Brown,* efforts by the executive branch and civil rights activists received legislative acknowledgment and support in the Civil Rights Act of 1964. A comprehensive piece of legislation, the Civil Rights Act of 1964 unequivocally declared that no person should be subjected to discriminatory treatment by any federal institution, program, activity, or grantee because of race, color, or national origin. The Act provided remedies for victims of discrimination by any institution covered by the Act, and directed federal agencies to issue rules and guidelines for achieving compliance with the Act.

The Civil Rights Act of 1964 was followed by the Voting Rights Act of 1965. The Act prohibited the use of literacy tests to qualify voters and abolished poll taxes— both of which had been used for many years to prevent blacks from voting. The Act proved to be a powerful weapon in the civil rights struggle to bring blacks political equality.

The Civil Rights Act of 1964 and the Voting Rights Act of 1965 were inspired by statistics that showed that racial discrimination was still the rule, not the exception, in voting, employment, education, and public accommodations. Previous efforts to eradicate racial discrimination had not been sufficient.

A final piece of civil rights legislation of importance, the Fair Housing Act of 1968, proscribed discrimination based on race, color, religion, national origin, or sex in the sale, rental, or financing of housing covered by the Act.

Passage of the equal opportunity legislation of the 1960s was a significant accomplishment in civil rights. It soon became apparent, however, that to treat as equals those who had for years been treated unequally was not sufficient; affirmative action would be needed to offset past imbalances and injustices.

This conclusion led to a number of executive orders, issued between 1965 and 1969. The cumulative effect of the orders was to require that the federal government, and its agencies, contractors, and subcontractors, take affirmative action to seek out and recruit qualified members of minority groups.

The equal opportunity and affirmative action laws of the 1960s and early 1970s gave civil rights leaders and supporters new ammunition with which to attack discriminatory policies. The example of the movement to attain civil rights for black Americans inspired similar activity by women, Hispanics, Native Americans, and other disadvantaged groups, such as the physically handicapped, the aged, the young, the homosexual, and the imprisoned. The civil rights movement accelerated and broadened to include an effort to obtain equal opportunities for all.

Just as the number of people seeking access to the American mainstream increased, however, the rate of economic growth declined, meaning that fewer opportunities were available. White men began to fear that they were at a disadvantage when competing against equally qualified minority applicants for educational, employment, housing, and other opportunities. This fear lay behind a "reverse discrimination" claim that appeared in many places in the nation in the 1970s. The "reverse discrimination" claim asserted that affirmative action remedies worked unfairly to the harm of the majority. The assertion had a chilling effect on affirmative action efforts, and had slowed these efforts considerably by the end of the 1970s.

The Present Climate

Progress has been made in the field of civil rights, but the United States has yet to realize its egalitarian ideal. Civil rights action has been deferred while the country addresses what are thought to be problems of higher importance. The present call for fiscal restraint has resulted in some program cancellations and has spread benefits more thinly among blacks, the poor, senior citizens, the young, and other disadvantaged program recipients, while the military budget will increase. Resistance to affirmative action has brought gains in employment and education to a virtual standstill.

Many Americans are unaware of the real dangers to civil rights in employment, in voting, in housing and education. As the following pages will show, the nation cannot afford to be complacent.

Employment

In the field of employment, prejudice and discrimination have had debilitating effects on the lives of those discriminated against. Without a national commitment to making whole the victims of systematic employment discrimination, these evils may never be mitigated. The experience of the black American in the labor force over the past 200 years has cast him into the worst paid, least desirable jobs

11

on the market. Although some progress has been made in recent decades, the consequences of institutional discrimination against black workers remain manifest.

The years immediately following the Civil War were marked by overt discrimination against the black worker and his consequent exclusion from the labor market. In the skilled crafts, in the mines and factories, and on the docks, whites gradually moved in and blacks left. The skilled slave—and there were many more skilled salves than is commonly recognized—had been protected by his politically more powerful master; but that protection was withdrawn after emancipation. With the rise of craft unionism and the apprentice system between 1865 and 1885, white artisans consolidated their hold on the jobs formerly held by blacks.

Technological changes contributed to this trend by making the skills of blacks increasingly obsolete, and by often rendering the work less strenuous and dirty, thus encouraging the definition of former "Negro jobs" as "white man's work." By 1900, a color-based caste system had become firmly entrenched. Blacks were almost completely segregated from the mainstream of labor by law and custom.

Blacks who migrated to the North took the unskilled jobs available in steel mills, auto plants, road maintenance, laundries, the feed industry, and some branches of the garment trades. As a rule, these were the jobs that whites and immigrants had left or did not want.

The entry of blacks into the Northern labor market was hampered by the prevailing racial attitudes of the early 20th century. White workers strongly resented the newcomers, especially because many of the black workers had been brought to the North by employers to be used as strikebreakers or as cheap labor.[5] The hostility and aggression of the white workers took on many forms. Blacks were victimized and terrorized by riots and other acts of violence. In 1917 and 1919, tensions between the two groups erupted into some of the most bitter and bloody race riots in this country's history.

These open and covert practices of excluding black workers had the net effect of securing for white workers the advantages of job security and economic advancement.

This history of discrimination was the reason for the enactment of Title VII of the Civil Rights Act of 1964. In enacting Title VII, Congress ordered "the removal of artificial, arbitrary, and unnecessary barriers to employment" when the barriers operate invidiously to discriminate on the basis of racial or other impermissible classification. Further, Title VII was designed to benefit persons who had been denied an equal opportunity to earn an equal paycheck. To effect this, Congress "vested broad equitable discretion in federal courts to order such affirmative action as may be appropriate. . . ."[6]

The Civil Rights Act of 1964 was indeed a major victory for civil rights leaders and supporters. Many felt that Title VII would enable blacks and members of other minority groups in the labor force to reach parity with their white counterparts. Statistics reveal, however, that a gross disparity between the incomes of white men and minority workers remains. National leadership is necessary to bring about a national commitment to close the employment gap.

In 1960, the unemployment rate for white men was 4.7 percent. Among black men the unemployment rate officially reached 8.6 percent, and among Puerto Rican men, 8.8 percent. The unemployment rate for white women was 4.7 percent. For black and Puerto Rican women, these rates were even higher—9.0 percent and 11.1 percent, respectively.

In 1970, 6 years after the passage of the Civil Rights Act of 1964, the employment figures for blacks, women, and members of minority groups were remarkably similar to the employment figures of 1960. Unemployment among white men was 3.6 percent; among black men, 7.1 percent were unemployed, and 6.3 percent of Puerto Rican men were out of work. The unemployment rate for white women was 5.0 percent; the unemployment rates for black and Puerto Rican women were 8.4 percent and 9.3 percent.

Although the affirmative action mandate was in force, the 1976 employment figures showed no improvement. White men had an unemployment rate of 5.9 percent; 15.9 percent of black men were officially unemployed, as were 16.3 percent of Puerto Rican men. Unemployment among white women reached 8.7 percent; among black women, 18.9 percent; among Puerto Rican women, 22.3 percent.[7]

The official unemployment rate for all workers in the U.S. labor force was reported to be 7.6 percent in August, 1980. The unemployment rate for whites was 6.8 percent; for blacks, 13.6 percent; for Hispanics, 10.6 percent.[8] The black unemployment rate is twice as high as that for whites.

The statistics indicate the necessity of immediately and aggressively implementing the Humphrey-Hawkins Full Employment and Economic Growth Act to reduce the overall national unemployment level to 4 percent, consistent with "reasonable price stability."* To reduce the

---

* The Act reads in pertinent part:

The Congress hereby declares that it is the continuing policy and responsibility of the Federal Government to use all practicable means, consistent with its needs and obligations and other essential national policies . . . [to] promote useful employment opportunities, including self-employment, for those able, willing, and seeking to work, and promote full employment and production, increased (*Continued*)

13

shocking unemployment rate among black youth, the Youth Employment and Educational Initiatives plan and the Comprehensive Employment and Training Act should be fully funded. Job training programs should be encouraged, and the private sector should hire the chronically unemployed of the inner cities. Tax incentives, with firm guarantees that they will benefit the unemployed, should be used as a means of getting industry to locate in inner cities and employ inner city residents.

In the 1980s the executive branch must stress the importance of developing and implementing voluntary affirmative action plans that take race into consideration. As a public policy, affirmative action has been in existence since the 1960s, but the gap between the education and income levels of whites and blacks has not been closed. Parity has not been achieved.

Affirmative Action

To achieve parity in this decade, the nation must undertake affirmative measures. These programs must take race into account, for "the poisonous legacy of legalized oppression [was] based upon the matter of color [and] can never be adequately purged from our society"[9] with a color-blind remedy.

The legality of voluntary affirmative action programs was established in the 1970s by two Supreme Court decisions. In *Regents of the University of California* v. *Bakke,*[10] the Court held that race may be used as a factor in selecting students for admission to higher education institutions and other government programs. Thus, the Court upheld the use of race as a factor for designing remedial activities by public officials.

The *Bakke* decision has broad implications. If a court finds that illegal racial discrimination has taken place, that court has the authority to order affirmative action, including the use of goals and timetables, quota hiring and promotion, and teacher and pupil assignments, based on race. In certain circumstances, the affirmative action plans required by federal administrative agencies will carry similar authority. And if a federal, state, or local legislative body determines that racial exclusion has existed in a program, and passes a law requiring affirmative action plans that use quotas, the law will be held constitutional.[11]

After *Bakke,* the Court heard *United Steelworkers of America* v. *Weber.*[12] The Court was asked to determine the boundaries of Title VII of the Civil Rights Act of 1964 as

real income, balanced growth, a balanced Federal budget, adequate productivity growth, proper attention to national priorities, achievement of an improved trade balance through increased exports and improvement in the international competitiveness of agriculture, business, and industry, and reasonable price stability. . . .

applied to a voluntary affirmative action plan negotiated by a private employer and a labor union when there had been no specific showing of past discrimination by the employer. The Court held that Title VII does not forbid private employers and unions from voluntarily agreeing on *bona fide* affirmative action plans that consider race for the purpose of eliminating manifest imbalances in traditionally segregated job categories.

Guided by the *Bakke* and *Weber* decisions, the executive branch must scrupulously monitor affirmative action programs now in existence to ensure that they remain effective. The monitoring efforts must be aimed at more than increasing the number of blacks, Hispanics, women, and minorities in a particular labor force; the members of the protected class should also receive placement, salary, promotion and training opportunities, and other benefits to which they are entitled. Artificial barriers to equal employment opportunities must be identified and eradicated.

Voting

Before 1965, many blacks were denied the effective use of the ballot. With the passage of the 1965 Voting Rights Act, the franchise became more accessible to millions of black citizens who had been unjustly denied it through such means as poll taxes, literacy tests, and governmentally imposed discrimination. At the beginning of the 1980s, the most immediate issue facing the black community and those who support full equality is the protection and extension of this right to vote. The loss or diminution of this right will surely lead to the loss of other rights.

A serious threat to voting rights comes from a built-in defect in the Voting Rights Act. Key provisions were enacted on a temporary basis—originally for 5 years, subsequently extended by amendments in 1970 and 1975. These provisions prevent those states and political subdivisions that have a history of restricting voting from making changes in their voting laws or practices if such changes have the purpose or effect of discrimination. In order to retain the political power they have gained under the 1965 Act, blacks and other minorities need the extension of this protection beyond the present termination date of 1982. Should Congress fail to vote an extension, minority groups will suffer dilution of their votes in the redrawing of Congressional and state electoral districts that will occur as a result of the 1980 census and through changes in voting procedures.

A challenge to minority voting strength comes from the Supreme Court. The Court has an established history of strong support for the objectives of the 15th Amendment; the civil rights community, however, regards the

Supreme Court's action in the term just past as a retreat from this stance. In *White* v. *Regester*,[13] a lower federal court held that where the circumstances related to the voting process had a racially discriminatory impact, a violation of the 15th Amendment had been proven. In the more recent *Bolden* v. *City of Mobile, Alabama*,[14] decision, the Supreme Court held otherwise, requiring that "racial intent" in establishing a voting process must be proved before the electoral system will be held unconstitutional. The decision makes it more difficult for blacks and other minorities to set aside multimember legislative districts that prevent them from exercising their full political potential.

The Panel believes that a priority item on the Congressional agenda for the 1980s should be legislation that will reverse the effect of *Bolden* and establish proof of discriminatory racial effect as a sufficient basis for outlawing electoral districts that dilute voting strength.

In view of the danger to the political rights of minorities posed by judicial decisions and by a recurrent racist element in public opinion, Congress should act early and decisively to protect and extend the franchise. The elimination of pre-registration should be considered. If pre-registration is retained, the registration of secondary school students by school principals or other officials might be permitted. The passage of a Constitutional amendment banning literacy tests should also be considered.

Fair Housing

In the 1970s, there was little progress toward equality in housing. Too many dwellings in black and minority communities remain substandard, and too many of these substandard dwellings are of disproportionately high cost. Inflation and high interest rates have made it increasingly difficult for all, especially blacks and minorities, to purchase homes. Federal efforts to develop and renovate existing black and other minority communities have resulted in widespread displacement.

In the 1980s efforts must address the housing problems of the ghetto in such a way that residents are not forced to move. Programs to promote black, female, and minority ownership of land and housing must be strengthened.

The direction fair housing enforcement will take in this decade depends in large measure on efforts by the executive branch to strengthen and enforce the Fair Housing Act of 1968 and the 1974 and 1977 Housing and Community Development Acts. Enforcement of the Fair Housing Act was virtually nonexistent in the 1970s because the Act had been stripped of key enforcement provisions. The

16

Department of Housing and Urban Development (HUD) now has only the authority to conciliate when investigation of a complaint shows probable discrimination; HUD has no authority to take action against private discriminators. For 10 years HUD failed to promulgate Title VIII regulations, another factor that has hindered the enforcement of the Act.

Congressional action to amend the Fair Housing Act to provide for administrative enforcement is now under way. An amendment proposed in the 96th Congress, H.R. 5200, is an essential step toward the effective enforcement of the Fair Housing Act. The Panel urges the passage and aggressive implementation of an equivalent bill in future legislative sessions.

Efforts to implement the 1974 and 1977 Housing and Community Development Acts have been weak. Members of minority groups and female heads of households, the intended beneficiaries of the Acts, have not profited to the extent that Congress intended. Despite attempts to rectify the deficiencies of the Acts, several critical weaknesses remain. Foremost is the need to protect low-income families from displacement caused by neighborhood revitalization and economic development activities. Standards must also be established for selecting sites for subsidized housing, and a procedure that enables eligible tenants to obtain standardized housing anywhere in a metropolitan area should be developed.

Women's Concerns

As a result of black Americans' movement for legal, economic, and educational equality, a women's movement emerged during the 1960s that produced substantial changes in federal and state laws in the 1970s. Efforts to ratify the Equal Rights Amendment were intensified, and public policy changes occurred in the areas of "credit, domestic violence, housing, marriage, rape, and abortion."[15]

In the 1980s, the executive branch should make every effort to secure a position of equality for women in the United States.

The historical position of women in American society has been one of second-class citizenship. According to an idealized conception of American life, men and women were partners in the enterprise of life. Men participated in the labor force; they were supposed to act competitively and aggressively. Women ran the home and raised the children; they were to act with a submissive and passive gentility. This ideal was less often practiced than honored, but it conditioned public policy as well as private opinion.

When women entered the labor force, as they did with some frequency, employers often decided that female workers needed special protection. The first women who worked in factories had special dormitory accommodations, on the theory that adult women required paternal protection. The first minimum wage laws in this country applied only to women. Some states and firms accompanied this legislation with other rules that applied exclusively to women, such as regulations that required pregnant women to remain away from the job for a certain period of time.

Until World War II, women were thought to work for "pin money" to supplement their father's or husband's wages. According to the theory, women worked only until they married, with the exception of a small group of women who had made a conscious decision not to marry. These career women tended to concentrate in the so-called genteel occupations, such as schoolteaching.

World War II marked the turning point in the nation's attitudes toward working women. Female labor force participation rose dramatically and continued to rise after the war. For the first time this rise was measured among white women as well as black, and among married women with children as well as women without children. Most girls born after the war grew up with the model of a working woman before them, and this change in role models helped to support the rise in the number of women who worked.

During the past 55 years, the numbers of women workers have risen from 1 out of every 5 workers to about 2 out of 5. Today, women compose more than 41 percent of the total labor force.[16] About one-eighth of all women workers are "minority race."[17] Despite the passage of the Equal Pay Act, fully employed women continue to earn less than do fully employed men. In 1967, the average income for fully employed men was $7,512; for black men, the average income was $5,069. Fully employed white women averaged $4,394, while minority women earned only $3,363. In 1977, the average income of fully employed white males was $15,230; black males, $11,053; white women, $8,787; and minority women, $8,385. Not only do fully employed women continue to earn less than fully employed men, but women remain under-represented as managers and skilled crafts workers. Only 6 percent of crafts workers are women; they hold only 23 percent of the managerial positions, and 23 percent of the nonretail sales positions.[18]

In the 1980s, equal pay for work of comparable value must become more than a slogan—it must become a reality of the American labor market. The nation's businesses and government agencies must consider substantial revision of wages when these wages reflect sexual stereotypes. For example, more than 80 percent of women workers are segregated in "women's" occupations that differ in content from "men's" jobs but in many cases do not differ in the skill, effort, and responsibility required. The Equal Employment Opportunity Commission (EEOC) could be called upon to determine whether appropriate job measurement procedures exist, or can be developed, to reevaluate "women's" jobs according to their real worth, so that the wage rate paid will truly reflect skill, effort, responsibility, and working conditions.

Job inequities that result from sexism and racial discrimination, like all other inequities, must be corrected. The necessary restructuring must begin now.

Changes in workplaces across the nation must proceed with the knowledge that corporate personnel practices were created by men, for men. In the design of white-collar jobs, for example, companies assumed that wives and children would move willingly. Fringe benefit programs, also, benefited men disproportionately. These practices did not meet the needs of women; parental and child care provisions were and are inadequate and equal monthly retirement benefits for women (whose life expectancies exceed those of men) have yet to be widely provided. These issues remain for the 1980s.

Increasing numbers of women are entering the labor market, and the need for child care is growing. In 1979, 45 percent of all women with children under the age of 6 were in the labor force, with an estimated 7.2 million preschool children in need of child care services.[19] As more mothers enter the labor force, the gap between the number of children and available child care facilities will continue to widen. Employers have shown little interest in providing day care centers for their employees. The cost of private facilities takes so high a percentage of the working mother's paycheck that it may not be worth her while to continue working. Some unions and a few hospitals have established day care centers, but these are too few in number to fill the demand. There is a clear need for the federal government to continue to provide funds and incentives for child care centers.

The Equal Employment Opportunity Commission must continue to make efforts to end employment practices that abuse women. The definition and prosecution of sexual harassment on the job stand out as important issues for the 1980s.

The job of the EEOC and other government agencies will be made much easier if the legal status of women is clarified. To guarantee the equal rights of women under the law, the nation should complete the matter of enacting the Equal Rights Amendment.

The 92nd Congress overwhelmingly approved the proposed Equal Rights Amendment, which provides in pertinent part: "Equality of rights under the law shall not be denied or abridged by the United States or by any State on account of sex." Thirty-eight states must approve this amendment before it can take effect; 35 states have done so. Congress has extended the deadline for ratification to June 30, 1982. In the first years of the 1980s, therefore, a concerted effort should be made to encourage at least three more states to ratify the Equal Rights Amendment.

Another issue that must be addressed early in the decade is abortion—the right of a women to end a pregnancy before it has come to term. The Panel opposes any attempt to make access to medical services contingent upon income. Health insurance for the poor should not be used to enforce ethical judgments about medical services.

Hispanics

Hispanics—people of Spanish origin—are one of the fastest-growing minority groups in the United States. The Bureau of the Census estimates that there are now 12 million Americans of Spanish origin living in this country.[20] Because of geographical distribution, language characteristics, and a number of socioeconomic factors shared by other minority groups, Hispanic Americans do not live life on equal terms with the majority. In March 1978, for example, the median income of non-Hispanic families was $16,300; Puerto Rican families had a median income of $8,000, less than half of the non-Hispanic figure.[21]

The Hispanic community comprises many different smaller communities. Of the Hispanic population of 12,046,000 in 1978, more than half were of Mexican origin, but there were also significant numbers of Cubans, Puerto Ricans, and other Latin Americans.[22]

Some groups seem to be more fortunate than others. The median income of Cuban families, for example, is about $14,200, compared with $11,400 for all families of Spanish origin. Still, the figures speak for themselves; they tell of a community that does not get its full share of opportunities. The poverty figures are particularly stark: roughly one-fifth of Hispanic families have incomes below the poverty line, more than double the non-Hispanic percentage.

Three demographic factors compound the problems of the Hispanic community. This group is perhaps the most urbanized in the United States. More than 80 percent of the Hispanic population lives in cities, and nearly half live in central cities. The Hispanic community is younger than the population as a whole, with a median age about 7.5 years below that of the rest of the population. Finally, a high degree of geographic concentration characterizes the Hispanic population. More than half of this population resides in Texas and California, and about 13 percent lives in New York. The Southwestern states and New York together account for nearly three-quarters of the Hispanic population in the United States.

The Hispanic community has much in common with blacks and women; measures that seek to end poverty will be of benefit to all three groups. Job training and youth initiative measures will help Hispanics as they will help other minority groups. However, the Hispanic community does have needs that differ from those of the rest of the population.

Hispanics derive their cultural heritage from countries that have a special historical relationship with the United States. In the case of Mexico, the bonds with the United States stem from a common border. Both Puerto Rico and Cuba trace their existence as modern political entities to the Spanish-American War at the turn of this century. The opportunities of the U.S. labor market and its nearness have prompted extensive immigration to the United States from Mexico and other Latin American countries. This immigration has led to the abuse of the civil rights of Hispanics.

The Immigration and Naturalization Service (INS) has the authority to deport undocumented aliens. The INS sometimes abuses this power, and other law enforcement agencies frequently usurp the INS mandate. As a result, Mexican-Americans are often stopped on roadways, or jailed, because of their appearance. This violation of due process is a denial of the civil rights of Mexican-Americans; it requires immediate redress. Congress should consider drafting strict guidelines that will protect the civil rights of Mexican-Americans in this country.

A second, related issue concerns the claims that undocumented aliens hold on U.S. social services. In the case of *Doe* v. *Plyler,* it was held that the children of undocumented aliens need not pay tuition to attend American public schools.[23] Although these children have a right to receive public education, their rights with regard to welfare and health care benefits remain unclear. The resolution of this matter may be one of the country's most important tasks in the coming years.

A broader question centers on the rights of non-English-speaking groups in the United States. As a general matter, the Panel believes that this country's language must be English. People who lack the ability to speak English, on the other hand, must not have their rights abridged for that reason alone. Agencies that enforce civil rights and dispense social services must make their services accessible to non-English-speaking Americans.

Communities with large numbers of non-English-speaking residents should consider the establishment of English-language instruction centers, perhaps located in neighborhood schools. For those who work, instruction could be scheduled in a school or another community center during the evening.

The Panel wishes to reemphasize that Hispanics have concerns that are identical to those of other minority groups. Matters of importance for the Hispanic community are also of concern to blacks, other minorities, and women; comments about unemployment rates or housing segregation apply with equal force to all of these constituencies. Likewise, the remedies available to members of one group (notably affirmative action) are available to all groups.

Conclusion

In this nation there must be a continuing commitment to ensuring the rights and welfare of blacks, women, Hispanics, members of other minority groups, and the poor. The current resurgence of conservative and reactionary sentiments throughout the nation must not be allowed to bring on a period of retrenchment, inaction, and retrogression with respect to civil rights that would negatively affect these groups.

This Panel believes that there must be an active commitment to full equality for all Americans. The ideals of America have not been met; the promise of America remains.

1. *Slaughter House Cases,* 83 U.S. 36 (1876).
2. *Dred Scott* v. *Sanford,* 60 U.S. 393 (1856).
3. *Plessy* v. *Ferguson,* 163 U.S. 537 (1896).
4. *Brown* v. *Board of Education of Topeka,* 347 U.S. 483 (1954).
5. Marshall, *The Negro and Organized Labor* (New York, 1965).
6. *Griggs* v. *Duke Power Co.,* 401 U.S. 424 (1971); *Albemarle Paper Co.* v. *Moody,* 422 U.S. 405, 417-425 (1975); *Franks* v. *Brown Transportation Co.,* 42 U.S. 747, 763 (1975).
7. U.S. Commission on Civil Rights, *Social Indicators of Equality for Minorities and Women* (Washington, D.C., 1978), p. 30; U.S. Department of Labor, Bureau of Labor Statistics, "The Employment Situation: 1980," mimeographed (Washington, D.C., September 1980).
8. "The Employment Situation."
9. A. Leon Higgenbotham, Jr., *In the Matter of Color: Race and the American Legal Process: The Colonial Period* (Oxford, 1978).
10. *Regents of the University of California* v. *Bakke,* 438 U.S. 265 (1978).
11. Nathaniel R. Jones, General Counsel, National Association for the Advancement of Colored People (NAACP), transcript, NAACP *Bakke* symposium, July 21, 1978.
12. *United Steelworkers of America* v. *Weber,* 443 U.S. 193 (1979).
13. *White* v. *Regester,* 422 U.S. 935 (1975).
14. *Bolden* v. *City of Mobile, Alabama,* 571 F.2d 238 (Fifth Circuit, 1978).
15. Galvin and Mendelsohn, "The Legal Status of Women," in *The Book of the States, 1980-1981* (Council of State Governments, 1980), p. 36,
16. U.S. Department of Labor, Office of the Secretary, Employment Standards Administration, Women's Bureau, *Women Workers Today* (Washington, D.C., 1976), p. 2.
17. *Ibid.,* p. 5, n. 1.
18. Prepared by the Women's Bureau of the U.S. Department of Labor from data published by the Bureau of the Census, U.S. Department of Commerce, August 1979.
19. U.S. Department of Commerce, Bureau of the Census, *Current Population Reports: Population Characteristics,* series P-20, no. 336 (Washington, D.C., 1979), p. 42.
20. The U.S. Commission on Civil Rights has asserted that Hispanics are seriously undercounted in all Census surveys, and that their numbers are considerably greater than those reported. See *Counting the Forgotten: The 1970 Census Count of Persons of Spanish Speaking Background in the United States* (Washington, D.C., 1974).
21. U.S. Department of Commerce, Bureau of the Census, *Current Population Reports: Population Characteristics,* series P-20, no. 339 (Washington, D.C., 1979), p. 1.
22. *Ibid.* The 1978 statistics indicate that 7 million Hispanic Americans are Mexican American; 1.8 million are Puerto Rican; 0.9 million are Central or South American; 0.7 million are Cuban; and 1.5 million are listed as "other Spanish."
23. *Doe* v. *Plyler,* 458 F.Supp. 569 (E.D. Tex. 1978).

Chapter 2

National
Health Policy
FOR THE 1980s

The government's role in health services has grown rapidly in the past 50 years, largely because of efforts to ensure access to health care for the poor and the elderly. The government is now directly responsible for paying for 40 percent of the nation's health care, principally through the federal Medicare program for the elderly and the state-run Medicaid program for the poor. How health care is paid for helps to determine which, and how, services are produced, and the influence of government programs and policies has been felt throughout the health care system.

In the 1980s, reform of the health care system must consider the nature of the services being offered as well as the question of how to finance such care. The Panel has concentrated its examination of health policy issues in the following areas:

☐ The financing of health care through national health insurance, which will encourage efficient production of high quality health care, accessible to the entire population;

☐ The increased role of disease prevention and health promotion efforts to eliminate causes of illness, disability, and early death where possible and to reduce the inequitable burdens of illness across population groups, where outright eradication of such illness is not possible; and

☐ The provision of health services and other kinds of care to the elderly in their homes and communities to reduce the present undue reliance on institutional forms of care.

Financing Care: National Health Insurance

Rarely has a public issue generated so much public enthusiasm and political debate, and produced so little legislative action, as has the idea of national health insurance. The public has favored some form of national health insurance program for more than 30 years. In 1979, pollsters Yankelovich, Skelly, and White found that 58 percent of the American public favored national health insurance.[1] Congress has responded to this public interest, scheduling hearings and introducing a variety of insurance proposals since 1938. In spite of this, the United States still lacks comprehensive government financing of health care.

National health insurance was originally proposed only to provide health insurance for the uninsured, who are vulnerable to financial ruin. But some see the issue more broadly, as a chance to construct a comprehensive social program that will address a number of deficiencies in the present health care system. This lack of agreement on the objectives of national health insurance has produced a wide spectrum of policy alternatives and is a major reason for the failure to enact any of them.

The public's main reason for supporting national health insurance appears to be concern over the inability of many to afford private health insurance, an inability that now limits access to adequate health care. A second reason is the hope that national health insurance might lower the costs of health care. It is also thought that the fragmentation of the present health care system might be reduced. Because of the way in which doctors and hospitals are presently organized, individual segments of the system often provide technologically advanced care, but these components often fail to work together in a way that provides high quality, continuous care.

National health insurance, therefore, appears as a multifaceted program that will address the necessity of improving health insurance coverage, increasing access to care, reducing health care costs, and improving the efficiency of the health care system.

Health Insurance Coverage

More than two-thirds of all health expenditures are now covered by some form of insurance. In 1950, only one-third of expenditures were covered, and as late as 1960, the percentage was still less than half.

Those without health insurance coverage are the poor, the young, and the unemployed. Figure 1 compares the percent distribution of the population across these dimensions with the distribution of the uninsured population. If health insurance were distributed equally across all population groups, the two proportions would be the same for each group. The differences indicate the relative adequacy or inadequacy of insurance within each.

Figure 1A demonstrates the extent to which the uninsured are over-represented among the poor. The converse, of course, is that the relatively affluent (with 1976 incomes exceeding $15,000) are far less likely to be uninsured.

The age distribution of insurance coverage, shown in Figure 1B, is more complex. Two significant gaps appear,

Figure 1
Characteristics of the Population and the Uninsured, 1976

A. Income

less than $5,000

$5,000 to $9,999

$10,000 to $14,999

$15,000 or more

B. Age

less than 6 years

6 to 18 years

19 to 24 years

25 to 44 years

45 to 64 years

65 years and over

C. Employment Status

Employed

    Full-time wage earner

    Part-time wage earner

    Self-employed

Unemployed

Not in Labor Force

    Retired

    Other

0   10% 20% 30% 40% 50% 60%

▨ Percent of the Total Population
■ Percent of the Uncovered

Figures are adjusted for underreporting of coverage by public programs. Totals may not equal 100 percent because of rounding.

Source: SIE 1976, *as cited in* Congressional Budget Office "Profile of Health Care Coverage: The Haves and Have-nots" (Washington, D.C. 1979)

among young adults and the elderly. People aged 19 to 24 constitute only 10.9 percent of the national population, but nearly 22 percent of the uninsured. For the elderly, the picture is reversed: those older than 65 are more than 10 percent of the population, but are only 1 percent of the uninsured. Medicare is almost wholly successful in providing the elderly with health insurance; the uninsured are those not included in the Social Security system.

Because health insurance is commonly available to employees as a fringe benefit, the employed tend to be well insured, as illustrated in Figure 1C. Not all the employed, however, are so fortunate; 12 percent of part-time workers and nearly 15 percent of self-employed people have no insurance. The unemployed are also over-represented among the uninsured.

There are three distinct groups outside of the labor force—children, retired people, and those who are not looking for work. Retired people are usually elderly; most receive Medicare and only 2 percent are uninsured. Of members of the other groups, however, 11 percent are uninsured.

Most health insurance in the United States is private, provided through employers (Figure 2). The Congressional Budget Office (CBO) estimates that between 165 million and 170 million people were enrolled in private health insurance plans in 1976; 77 million were enrolled in or received services through government programs (Medicare, Medicaid, and the Veterans' Administration health system).[2]

The present health insurance system in this country covers a high proportion of the population, but distinct gaps are evident. Those less likely to have insurance belong to four groups:

- ☐ The unemployed who have lost employer-provided health insurance;
- ☐ The near-poor, who are unable to qualify for the means-tested Medicaid programs;*
- ☐ Young people who are uninsured dependents or who do not qualify for insurance because they are unemployed or employed in uncovered industries or occupations; and
- ☐ Part-time workers or the self-employed who, again, are not included in employee fringe benefit programs.

---

* Medicaid is a state program, with eligibility often limited to those eligible for the state's public assistance programs. Criteria for eligibility vary widely, and in some states the requirement is as low as one-half of the poverty income. For this reason over half of the poor in the country are not even eligible for Medicaid coverage.

Figure 2
Type of Insurance Coverage of the Population, 1976

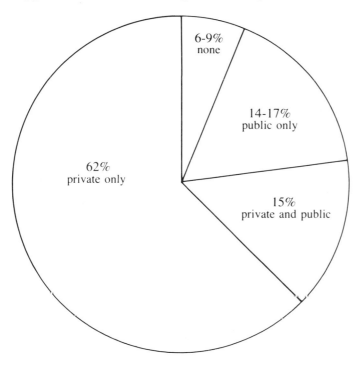

6-9%
none

14-17%
public only

62%
private only

15%
private and public

The lack of insurance is not the only problem arising from the present fragmented approach to health insurance. Many people have inadequate insurance that leaves them at risk of an economically catastrophic loss.

The Underinsured

Adequacy of coverage depends on health status, family income, and wealth, among other factors. The Congressional Budget Office provides an indication of the adequacy of insurance in terms of its ability to protect subscribers from high financial loss.[3] According to the CBO, the burden of medical expense is highly uneven. In fiscal year 1978, more than three-quarters of those under 65 incurred medical expenses of less than $100. However, the 1.3 percent of this group with expenses in excess of $5,000 spent more than 30 percent of all health expenditures. More than 21 million families (28 percent of all families) incurred medical expenses in excess of 15 percent of their gross income in 1978. Of course most of these families had health insurance that covered most of this expense; but 6.9 percent of these families had to meet out-of-pocket expenses that exceeded 15 percent of their gross income. Catastrophic medical expense is rare, but is an enormous burden on those affected.

In addition to this lack of adequate catastrophic coverage, existing health insurance policies are criticized for offering coverage that discourages the cost-efficient use of health services. Policies often exclude coverage for preventive care, providing instead coverage for curative care after a disease process is well under way. Some preventive services, it is true, are not cost-effective; but others are, and their use should be encouraged with financial incentives.

Uneven Coverage of Services

Frequently, entire categories of out-of-hospital care are not covered by insurance—the costs of dental services, prescribed drugs, and even physicians' services, for example, are either excluded from a reimbursement schedule, or are reimbursed less fully than are inpatient services. Some of these services, such as dental care, were originally thought to be less necessary and were traditionally excluded from health insurance coverage. The extent to which hospital and outpatient services can be substituted for one another is now much better understood, as are the benefits of preventive or early treatment. Both quality of care and cost considerations mandate that a wide variety of services should be included in any comprehensive national health insurance program; in this way, prompt, effective use of the least costly forms of appropriate medical care can be encouraged, rather than discouraged.

30

One measure of the access to needed health care is based upon the disparities in illness or death rates across geographic regions, ethnic groups, or income categories. Because the incidence or prevalence rates of most diseases are not medically related to these factors, observed variations must be attributable to the way in which the health system functions.

Unequal Access to Care

The maternal death rate, for example, is five times as high among blacks as among whites, and the infant mortality rate is nearly twice as high. Mortality rates for communicable diseases also vary across racial groups. There are five times as many deaths from tuberculosis among blacks as among whites, three times as many deaths from hypertension, twice as many from cirrhosis of the liver, and 60 percent more deaths from influenza.[4]

The most widespread medical problem in the United States is dental caries, which affects 98 percent of the population—and dentistry is the one health sector that can demonstrate unequivocal success through prevention. Poor people have four times as many untreated decayed teeth as do members of the middle and upper income groups. Forty-seven percent of children under 12 have never been to a dentist—and this is the very group that can benefit most from preventive care. Dental expenses, it will be remembered, are seldom reimbursed through health insurance policies.

The present health care system has grown largely in response to the way in which services have been purchased. Therefore, in order to understand better how any revised financing program might work, it will be useful to analyze how the present system works.

Health System Characteristics

Since the 1930s health insurance has been based upon cost or charge reimbursement, meaning that prevailing charges were generally accepted for payment by insurers. This arrangement has created a unique three-cornered market for medical care in which the traditional roles of "consumer" and "producer" are obscured. Although the patient receives a medical service, he does so under the recommendation and authorization of a physician; the patient rarely takes an active role in selecting the service to be purchased. Subsequently, a third party, the insurer, pays the bills. It is difficult, under this system, to find a traditional buyer of medical care. The patient receives treatment, but does not order the service, and the insurer pays the bill, leaving the patient only with an annually determined premium to pay. No one party is actually responsible for costs. It is not surprising that cost controls or cost restraints have been so difficult to achieve.

31

Most physicians and hospitals receive payment for each service rendered (so-called "fee-for-service" reimbursement). This practice encourages fragmented, specialty-oriented care, with each provider acting independently. There is no specific role for a coordinator of care—one who sees the patient as a whole person. This fragmentation can be detrimental to the patient, as when several physicians, not knowing of one another's actions, each prescribe medication for a patient's problem.

The acceptance of prevailing charges has reduced any incentive on the part of providers to lower costs to compete for patients. Seldom do either patients or insurers "comparison shop" by considering several prices for care. This encourages physicians and facilities to locate in wealthy sections, to the detriment of inner city and rural areas. Specialty distribution is equally skewed; many young physicians enter sophisticated specialties, but few undertake primary care training and enter general or family practice.

A different payment basis for health care, which attempts to address the deficiencies noted above, currently exists in many areas of the country. This approach is likely to increase in importance under a national health policy and should be considered carefully.

This approach is used by prepaid group practices, sometimes called health maintenance organizations (HMOs). Various forms of health maintenance organizations exist. In most, the medical group itself acts as the insurer, receiving the premium payment for coverage and, in return, agreeing to provide comprehensive health care, including ambulatory and hospital services. The provider group assumes the risk of high use and cost, and therefore has an incentive to economize in terms of the services provided and the cost of those services. Participating physicians are usually paid a fixed salary, rather than on a fee-for-service basis, and so have no economic incentive to authorize more care than is absolutely necessary. Because the plan must deliver all health care, including hospitalization, the economies of ambulatory care are utilized whenever possible and hospitals are used less often.

Two constraints protect health maintenance organization members from the dangers of receiving too little care. The first is that people enrolled in an HMO are members by choice; they are free to select a regular insurer should the organization's care be perceived as inadequate. A health maintenance organization that is not responsive to patients' needs will not stay in business for long. Second, a dissatisfied member may still resort to the usual legal remedy of a suit for malpractice.

Where health maintenance organizations have been in existence for a number of years, they have been broadly accepted and successful. In areas of the West Coast, for example, where these programs began, more than 20 percent of the population is enrolled in such groups.[5] The importance of the concept goes beyond the actual numbers, however; health maintenance organizations influence the prevailing pattern of care because they compete for the insurance subscriber's premium dollar.

Few would suggest that health maintenance organizations suit everyone. There are disadvantages, notably a restricted choice of physicians and hospitals. In addition, the utilization constraints on all services imply that some elective procedures are less likely to be authorized, and waiting lists for nonemergency hospital admissions tend to be longer than in the fee-for-service sector. The HMO model does, however, offer comprehensive, coordinated care, usually at an annual cost lower than that of a comparable fee-for-service full-coverage insurance plan. If a variety of systems coexist, competing with one another, it is to the public benefit.

Health Care Cost Inflation

The cost of health care has become a substantial burden to both the general public and the government. The growth in expenditures for health care in the United States is remarkable. In 1950 the nation spent $12.7 billion on health care; that was 4.5 percent of the gross national product (GNP). By 1960, the figure was $26.9 billion (5.3 percent of the GNP); by 1970, after the effects of Medicare and Medicaid were felt, expenditures had risen to $74.7 billion, or 7.6 percent of the GNP. It is expected that figures for 1980 will show that $244.6 billion (9.5 percent of the GNP), were spent on health care that year; and projections indicate that by the end of the decade health expenditures will be $757.9 billion, or 11.5 percent of the GNP. In per capita terms, expenditures have risen from $82 to $863 per year from 1950 to 1978. By 1990, projections indicate, each person will spend over $3,000 per year.[6]

A large part of this increase can be attributed to general inflation, but during most of this period the rise in the price of medical care was at least 50 percent greater than was the rise in the overall cost of living. In fact, between 1969 and 1978, personal health care expenditures rose by nearly 13 percent per year—substantially faster than the rise in the overall cost of living. The rise in intensity of care (as measured by the quantity of services being produced) accounted for approximately 25 percent of the rise in expenditures.

The shifting pattern in the source of payment for health care is as important to appreciate as are the changes in the price and quantity of services. In 1950, approximately one-third of health care expenditures was paid for by third parties (either private insurers or the government); by 1978, this proportion had doubled. Equally dramatic has been the rise in the government's share of this third-party financing. In 1950 the government was responsible for paying for approximately 22 percent of the health services purchased; by 1978, this share had risen to nearly 40 percent.

There is no doubt that these public expenditures for health threaten all other social programs, at both the state and the federal levels, especially in times of intense fiscal restraint. Some states have begun to reduce the burden of Medicaid by restricting program eligibility, thereby placing additional hardship on those least able to afford it. At the federal level, serious attempts have been made to control the costs of health care. Some have noted that the Medicare and Medicaid programs caused health care costs and expenditures to rise, and have suggested that expanded financing programs should await some evidence that the sector is under control as far as costs are concerned.

Several regulatory approaches to cost containment have been employed. Cost-sharing by patients is often suggested as a means of restraining demand for inessential services. Other approaches seek to reform the ways in which health services are supplied. Health planning, for example, is designed to reduce redundancy in capital equipment by limiting new investment expenditures to situations in which a clear need for the service can be demonstrated.

Another supply-side approach is to encourage more efficient delivery of services by using peer review to evaluate the quality and appropriateness of care by physicians and hospitals. A number of such programs have been successful in shortening the length of the average hospital stay, and "second opinion" programs appear to have reduced the incidence of unnecessary elective surgery.[7]

Still another policy option is to reimburse providers prospectively, that is, at a pre-determined rate before services are rendered. Prospective reimbursement encourages more efficient care because the provider shares the risk of additional costs of treatment; it reduces the temptation to over-treat patients. Critics point out, however, that prospective reimbursement does contain a perverse incentive to under-treat.

A characteristic common to all of these supply-side efforts to reduce costs is that they rely upon implementation at the local level, within a particular area or facility. Also, such plans often disturb or reverse traditional lines of authority among physicians, administrators, and the public. Not surprisingly, therefore, their success across the country has been uneven. Health planning has been very effective in a few locales, but ineffective in others. Some hospitals have implemented active and respected peer review programs, but others have been less willing to create these committees that intervene by questioning medical practices and procedures. Such programs can help to contain costs, but no one approach is likely to be equally effective in all settings—least of all if the regulatory program is designed at the federal level. Providers must be given an incentive to contain costs, but must be free to devise their own means of implementation. A successful national health insurance program must offer both the incentive to contain costs and the flexibility to implement different cost-containment efforts.

One of the major reasons for the controversy surrounding national health insurance is a lack of agreement on the underlying principles to which such a program should adhere. The Panel proposes the following criteria:

Criteria for National Health Insurance

- ☐ First, the national health insurance program should be equitable across all population groups. Adequate, appropriate health services must be available to all.
- ☐ Second, the program must encourage efficiency in both the production and consumption of health services. Appropriate incentives must be included to encourage patients to seek care at an early stage of illness, and for providers to select the least costly mode of appropriate care, including the use of less intensive forms of hospitals (such as day hospitals and ambulatory surgery programs) and staffing patterns (including the use of physicians' assistants and nurse practitioners).
- ☐ Third, all consumers of health care should be able to express their preferences as to the type of care they find most suitable. Government has a role in maximizing the amount of available information about options, so that choices can be made more intelligently.

Proposed reforms of the system follow three broad philosophies. The first assumes that the overall system is working acceptably, although access to insurance is not as broad as it should be. The suggested remedy is an extension of coverage to groups presently without health insurance, accompanied by the broadening of existing coverage to include catastrophic expenses. The advantage of this approach is that it is least disruptive of the existing system and would be the least costly of the proposed reforms. However, although this approach effectively addresses the inadequacy of the present distribution of health insurance,

Expansion

it fails to address other serious problems, and may in fact make them worse. This is especially true of the present reliance on highly technological, specialized forms of medical care, which operates to the detriment of primary, continuous care. Coverage of catastrophic expenses would do nothing to encourage the use of more efficient forms of care—it would actually do just the opposite, by guaranteeing reimbursement for the most expensive medical care.

The second path to reform is based on the assumption that the market for health care cannot work efficiently by itself, that it has characteristics that require regulation to ensure access, quality, and cost efficiency. If this strategy were followed, present attempts to ensure quality and contain costs (through utilization review, health planning, prospective reimbursement, and perhaps consumer cost-sharing) would be maintained and expanded. A likely mechanism for implementing these regulations could be a single comprehensive health insurance program that would require compliance from all participating providers. The single-plan approach may be essential if the regulatory elements are to be effective as they are now designed. *Regulation*

The advantages of this approach to national health insurance are many. A single insurance plan would ensure equity and would be a relatively simple organization to maintain. The results of experience with these regulatory programs, however, are not conducive to optimism. The present health care system is remarkably complex, and physicians have shown themselves to be adept at overcoming burdensome regulations. Programs that are designed to work well in one setting seldom work well in another. Furthermore, this regulatory system would foster more homogeneity than consumers might prefer, as all providers will necessarily adopt similar patterns of care, staff, and access.

Another regulated approach would be the creation of a national health service. According to its proponents, this plan would best achieve the desired reforms, because they would be inherent to the publicly owned system. Salaries and fees would be set by the government, facilities would be built and staffed according to a national plan, and access to all would be guaranteed. The success of the national health service in Great Britain is well known; it has achieved an enviable record in cost containment and a generally high level of acceptance by the British people. But a system of this kind implies such a radical restructuring of the medical sector that its implementation in the United States is neither feasible nor desirable.

An alternative to the regulatory strategy depends upon the forces of market competition to increase efficiency and heighten responsiveness to consumers' preferences. The competitive strategy relies on consumers' ability to choose for themselves the most appropriate health care plan if they receive information pertinent to the costs and benefits of each and an economic incentive to choose prudently. For some, economy is a paramount consideration; for others, convenience may be more important, or the ability to select a particular physician. Because consumers' preferences are so varied, the availability of many different provider and insurance systems would be most likely to maximize individual satisfaction.

It is often said that patients will not be intelligent shoppers in the health services market. Because they do not have the proper information, patients cannot readily compare the relative qualities of hospitals or physicians, nor can they evaluate clinical data as to the necessity of a particular procedure. The ability of consumers to choose health services rationally depends largely upon their particular circumstances. One could describe two types of consumers: one is well, can be informed, and is emotionally and physically capable of making rational choices, much as many employees do now when selecting among health insurance alternatives. A sick person, on the other hand, may be incapable of making such rational choices. It is important that the consumer choose the type of health care to be delivered before it is needed, rather than waiting until illness strikes.

Under these conditions consumers are able to evaluate choices, not on a procedure-by-procedure basis, but by comparing alternative insurance or delivery plans. Some insurers might offer a program that economizes by negotiating with physicians or hospitals over fees, for example, and may therefore be able to reduce the cost of insurance below that of another plan which would reimburse any qualified provider at prevailing rates. Another option would be membership in a health maintenance organization.

For many, especially those employed by the federal government or other large employers, a choice of insurance alternatives is presently available. Unfortunately, however, tax laws reduce actual competition in the health service market by encouraging employers to offer high-cost health insurance coverage as a fringe benefit. Workers who might prefer higher wages and a less expensive health care package are penalized (wages are taxable, but the employer's contributions to insurance premiums are not).

One advantage of a competitive national insurance program is that consumers' preferences are more likely to be met than would be the case if a single insurance plan were developed for the entire country. Competition will also encourage insurers and medical care providers to become more efficient and responsive to consumer preferences. Such regulations as are necessary can be designed to apply to particular groups of providers and insurance subscribers, instead of being forcibly applied across the board.

An important consideration in developing a national health financing program is that the poor and the elderly must be able to exercise market discretion, as the rest of society already does, in order to ensure quality of service. A common problem of social programs is that they segregate dependent groups into service systems that differ from those used by the middle class. A health insurance system must be developed that offers equality of access and the ability to purchase services from the provider who best meets individual preferences.

There are two different mechanisms for financing competitive health insurance programs through a national health insurance system. The first uses employers' contributions to purchase coverage for most subscribers; the other uses tax credits or other direct government transfers.

A Competitive Insurance System

In the first case, employers would be allowed to contribute a basic, tax-free amount toward an employee's health insurance. This sum would be equal to the cost of a modest insurance plan available in the community, typically one that would cover a wide range of specified services and that would have cost-containment features, perhaps including cost-sharing. If an employee preferred additional coverage, reduced cost-sharing, or other amenities of service not available through this basic plan, an expanded coverage option could be purchased through the employer. The additional cost would be borne by the employee, using "after-tax" dollars. Government financing of the basic insurance plan would be developed for those unemployed or out of the labor force. These people would also have the option of applying the government allocation toward a different insurance plan.

The second mechanism for financing basic health coverage for all Americans would use direct government transfers, such as tax credits issued to each person, regardless of his employment status. Under this plan everyone would be obliged to enroll in one of a variety of health insurance plans. If one chose to use one's credit toward purchasing more expensive coverage than that offered by the basic plan, the difference would be paid from one's after-tax income.

The Panel is of the opinion that either means of financing a competitive insurance program would be acceptable, as long as the consolidation of Medicaid and Medicare would be accomplished through a government-provided premium subsidy.

The competitive model of insurance works equally well whether the services covered in the basic plan are broad and comprehensive or relatively narrow. This decision will be based on the answer to one question: How costly a system can the nation afford at the time national health insurance is enacted? Fiscal constraints may suggest a more limited range of coverage in the beginning, with other services to be added gradually. It is crucial to the efficiency of the health care system that initial coverage be complete enough, that the bias toward expensive hospital care, as opposed to less expensive ambulatory care, be corrected. Similarly, consideration should be given to covering the costs of outpatient drugs, which often serve as a substitute for either ambulatory or hospital care; of dental care; and of programs that offer day care and homemaker services, which can often substitute for nursing home care.

The design of the basic health insurance program must not be used as the vehicle for making difficult social and ethical decisions. If a particular service, such as abortion, is covered by an expanded insurance plan, its omission from the basic plan on moral grounds would itself be immoral. Moral decisions must not be applied differentially across economic groups. All people are entitled to high quality health care services.

The financing mechanisms described above illustrate one of the more serious difficulties that have impeded the passage of national health insurance—the question of the cost of the program to the federal treasury. If employers' contributions were used, the major cost of health insurance would be borne by the private sector, and would therefore not appear directly as government expenditures. Tax credits or other subsidies, on the other hand, are paid directly by the government; the apparent cost of the tax credit plan is thereby higher than that of the employer contribution plan. With the need for balanced budgets and fiscal restraint in the 1980s so widely accepted, this distinction seems vital.

In reality, however, employers' contributions are tax-exempt. In addition, employers' contributions to fringe benefits are paid in lieu of wages; requiring employers to bear this expense reduces net wages to the same extent as would a government payment. The effect on individuals is the same. There may be some reduction in administrative costs if one government agency were to arrange for health insurance premiums for every person in the country. And even with a major role for employers, there would still be public provision of insurance for those not covered by employer plans. The difference in cost between the public or private provision of health insurance to all Americans, therefore, is more apparent than real.

For a number of reasons, estimating the costs of health insurance programs presents difficulties. The most important of these is that it is not accurately known how consumers would respond to the different prices associated with the various insurance alternatives. Although estimates of the price sensitivity of medical care have been made, these estimates are not specific for types of patients or services; and even if short-term utilization levels could be predicted, long-term rates cannot be. Long-term response patterns are especially important when the effects of increased use of preventive services are taken into account.

A second complication is that health insurance proposals are highly complex; they vary by the population enrolled, the services covered, the method of reimbursement, and the extent of patient cost-sharing. In addition, all proposals are linked to other policies, including health cost controls, and to other insurance programs designed for the poor, the elderly, children, and veterans. How the linkages are formed will determine the cost of any proposed program.

The Department of Health and Human Services estimates that a catastrophic insurance plan would be relatively inexpensive.* Such a plan would increase current health spending by approximately $3 billion, calculated in 1980 dollars for the 1980 population. The burden of the increase would be on the federal government; individuals would reduce their spending significantly.[8]

Estimates developed for the Carter Administration's 1980 program, one type of regulated system, suggest that expenditures would rise by about $14 billion.[9] This proposal incorporates the Medicare and Medicaid programs, but leaves insurance for the employed in the private sector, relying principally upon employers' contributions for financing. Both federal and employer expenditures would rise substantially, and individual expenditures would fall. (These estimates assume the success of the cost controls that form part of the proposal.)

The probable costs of the proposals that rely on competition are the most difficult to estimate because the bills differ so widely in terms of the basic insurance package, the specific tax treatment of premium contributions, and the size of the premium subsidy. Because of these complexities, and because the idea is so new, cost estimates have not yet been made. One could, however, approximate the costs by considering the separate components of a proposal. Such a national health insurance system would, at a minimum, finance health insurance for the poor and elderly, and leave the financing of insurance for the

---

* Such a plan would place a particular burden on minority communities and on the poor, who lack even a little money to pay for health care.

employed and their dependents to the private sector. Another aspect that has considerable cost implications is the increased use of relatively efficient insurers, such as health maintenance organizations. The estimated savings from that shift should be deducted from the estimated direct costs.

The $14 billion cost estimate developed for the Carter Administration's proposal could be used to estimate the direct financing cost of a consolidated Medicaid, Medicare, and Supplemental Security Insurance (SSI) program that would also remedy some of the deficiencies of coverage discussed above. The savings that would result from increased efficiency—as difficult as those are to predict—should be deducted from this estimate.

The Congressional Budget Office has attempted to estimate these savings.[10] They are thought to range from $2.5 billion to $7.5 billion, depending in part upon the specific tax treatment of insurance premiums. The net cost of the program in 1980 dollars, therefore, would range from $6.5 billion to $11.5 billion.

The U.S. health financing system has created a health care sector that is respected worldwide for its advanced technology. Yet it is so arranged as to provide acute care when preventive services are needed, specialty care when primary care is needed, an abundance of care in urban areas and a shortage in rural areas, and an inflationary spiral in health care costs that regulatory approaches seem unable to control.

Guaranteeing access to high quality health care services is an essential element in the health policy agenda for the 1980s. A complementary goal is to ensure that the kinds of services provided are well matched to the needs of the population. The following sections of this chapter discuss two areas in which considerable improvement can be made in the quality of health services, while the reliance upon costly, capital-intensive forms of medical care is reduced.

The role of prevention in medical care is not new. The nation's earliest public health activities resulted in improved water and sanitation systems to prevent the spread of infectious diseases. Many other diseases, including poliomyelitis, measles, and rubella, have been successfully fought by preventive immunization programs. Chronic diseases, however, have become major causes of disability and death. People who once were at risk from infectious diseases such as typhoid and cholera are now more likely to live to an age at which they are susceptible to cancer or heart disease. More important than "competing risk" as a cause of the increased incidence of these illnesses are such factors as environmental conditions and choice of life styles, which are now understood to be closely associated with illness.

Prevention and Equity in Health Care

Treatment of chronic disease has been accomplished only at an enormous social cost, and the success stories, although sometimes dramatic, have not been numerous. The nation has lost sight of the potential for using preventive measures to reduce the burden of heart disease, cancer, stroke, and other major causes of disability and death. These possibilities must be reconsidered in the 1980s.

Disease prevention will in the long run be based upon the findings of medical research. Once a disease is understood well enough to be prevented, the costs of eradication are often far less than those of the intermediate, half-way technologies employed to save sufferers' lives. It is only necessary to consider the terrible price paid by polio victims confined to iron lungs, and compare that to the vaccines in use today, to prove this point. Some day kidney dialysis and transplantation too will be seen as only steps leading to the cure and prevention of kidney disease.

Targets of Prevention

There are three strategies for applying preventive techniques to major health care problems while serving the cause of social justice. The first is, very simply, preventing those causes of illness or death that can be prevented with current knowledge and technology. Infectious diseases such as measles, mumps, and poliomyelitis, and many deaths from cervical cancer, for example, are clearly preventable through the wider application of known methods.

The second strategy is the use of disease prevention techniques to reduce the disparities in health conditions across geographic, ethnic, educational, or income categories. For most illnesses there is little medical or biological reason for the current differences in morbidity and mortality rates across these population groups. These disparities can certainly be reduced or eliminated, although it may not be possible to eradicate the diseases themselves.

The third strategy is directed toward reducing the incidences of illnesses or deaths whose causes are apparently related to environmental agents or life style characteristics. Although the fundamental, biological causes of these diseases are unknown, the probability of contracting such illnesses as lung cancer and heart disease can be reduced, as can the odds of dying in an automobile accident.

Great progress has been made in eliminating many diseases. For example, the development of immunization procedures led to a decline in the number of deaths due to diphtheria from 15,000 annually in the 1920s to only 7 in 1976. Cases of poliomyelitis fell from 21,000 in 1952 to only 4 in 1978. Since World War II a number of other

Preventable Disease

infectious diseases have virtually disappeared from the United States.

Despite this progress in combating disease, concern remains. The causal agents of these diseases have not been eradicated; continued vigilance is necessary to prevent them from becoming serious public health problems once more. Most of the cases reported today could have been prevented had immunization been available and encouraged for every child in the country. In some areas only 50 percent of 2-year-olds now complete the basic immunization series. Ten percent of children entering school for the first time are not fully immunized, and follow-up immunizations are not always received.

Immunization is an example of a preventive technique that is known to work, is easily administered, and is, for the most part, available. Yet not everyone takes advantage of this technology. Such effective prevention measures go unused because of poor public information programs and limited access to primary medical care.

There are distinct groups of people whose health differs substantially from that of the majority. Generally, these are the poor, the less educated, and the nonwhite. These groups rate lower on a wide range of health status indicators. They suffer from higher mortality rates, have lower life expectancies at birth, and are less confident about their own health. Acute and chronic disease conditions and risk factors leading to them are more common among these groups.

Equity Through Prevention

The age-adjusted mortality rate for minorities is 33 percent higher than the white rate. Mortality rates for tuberculosis, influenza, syphilis, and pneumonia are several times higher for poor blacks than for middle-class whites. Life expectancy at birth is 5 years longer for a white person than it is for a nonwhite, and the infant mortality rate for blacks is double that for whites. The maternal mortality rate for blacks is five times as high as that for whites. Blacks are three times as likely to die from high blood pressure as are whites, and five times as likely to die from tuberculosis. Nutritional deficiencies are more than six times as likely to cause early deaths among nonwhites as among whites; early deaths from anemias are five times as likely.[11]

A recent study notes that 28 percent of the United States population is likely to die before reaching the age of 65, a figure that places the nation 26th among the countries of the world. If the white and nonwhite populations were ranked separately, whites would still rank a relatively poor 19th, and nonwhites would rank a dismal 41st.[12]

Fifty percent of whites describe their health as excellent; only 36 percent of nonwhites say the same. This contrast is even more striking across income groups—65 percent of members of higher income groups report themselves in excellent health. This is true for only 32 percent of those in the lower income groups.

Cancer incidence and infant mortality rates are also inversely related to income, as are heart disease, diabetes, arthritis, emphysema, high blood pressure, and a number of other conditions. Persons in the lowest income group lose twice as many days of work due to illness as do persons in the highest group; they are also 350 percent more likely to be chronically disabled. This trend also holds for comparisons across educational levels, because educational attainment is correlated with both income and race.[13]

Comparisons of the poor with the nonpoor, the less educated with the educated, and the nonwhite with the white populations are characterized by wide variation on a number of measures of health and health status. Rarely do the differences in health status across race, education, or income have a medical basis; the differentials result from a complex relationship involving health attitudes and knowledge and access to health care services. Barriers to obtaining quality health care services are often serious for the disadvantaged because of economic, geographic, or cultural factors.

Differences in the availability or accessibility of services to certain groups of people will lead to different utilization rates among segments of the population. There is widespread agreement that the poor receive less medical care than the nonpoor, and that what they do receive is of lower quality. The Medicaid program has made notable progress in encouraging people to seek care, but it has not eliminated differences in the quality of available services. Efforts to contain health care costs often take the form of restrictions applied to the Medicaid and Medicare programs, which reduce the amount and quality of care available to those least able to support such a curtailment. Disease prevention efforts must acknowledge and address this disparity between the disadvantaged and the fortunate in order to lower disability and mortality rates among those who suffer most.

Other barriers to accessibility to health services among the disadvantaged must be attacked as well. Underutilization of medical services by poor people has been observed even when adequate services are available and physically accessible.

The attitudes of the poor, the less educated, and the nonwhite toward health and illness and toward the health care system are responsible for much of this underutilization. Cultural norms and lack of information seem to be the major determinants of these attitudes; the perceived overprofessionalization, impersonality, and middle-class orientation of the system are also significant. Cultural definitions of illness and cultural pressures play major roles in determining how one responds to symptoms and whether and when one seeks medical care. As a tragic result, members of low-income groups have higher hospital admission rates and longer lengths of stay, reflecting in part the sufferance of a greater severity of illness before medical care is sought.

Disadvantaged groups have a much higher prevalence of risk factors for diseases and they practice disease prevention to a lesser degree than do other groups. Far fewer nonwhite than white women seek prenatal care in the first trimester of pregnancy, fewer nonwhite than white children are immunized against infectious diseases, and many fewer poor children than rich see a dentist before the age of 12.

A great deal of the difference in health across population groups can be prevented by improving the accessibility and utilization of existing technologies. Programs such as national health insurance can not only ensure financial access to services, but can aid in the development of new health programs designed for the disadvantaged. The health education needs of the disadvantaged must be met so that they can better understand the nature of the health care system and learn how to use services available to them. The effectiveness of the health services system could be improved by providing appropriate care in inadequately served areas, by increasing the representation of minority groups among personnel, and by introducing new health practitioners within the primary health care system.

Prevention and Chronic Disease

The magnitude of the increase of chronic diseases in this country is reflected in the absolute rise in its incidence and in the greater proportion of deaths that such diseases cause. Between 1900 and 1970, rates of death due to infectious disease fell by 95 percent, but the rates of death due to cancer and heart disease rose by 250 percent. In 1900, 20 percent of deaths were attributed to cancer and heart disease combined; deaths due to tuberculosis and influenza totalled 22 percent. By 1940, however, the proportions were 50 and 10 percent, and by 1977, they were 70 and 3 percent, respectively. In 1980, more than 50 percent of early deaths in the United States were caused by heart disease and cancer.[14]

In the attempt to prevent the new leading causes of death, the focus has been on biomedical research into the causes of disease and on its early detection and treatment (secondary prevention methods), rather than on primary prevention related to life styles and behavior of individuals. Early detection and treatment is now seen as an approach of limited benefit. The American Cancer Society now recommends a more conservative schedule of screenings and tests in recognition of their high cost and limited success in treating those cases that are detected. Only recently has the primary prevention of chronic illness attracted attention, as may be seen by the fact that only 4 percent of federal health expenditures is devoted to disease prevention efforts. This figure is strongly indicative of a substantial commitment to treatment rather than prevention.

For thousands of individuals, treatment represents the only hope of survival from illness. One could hardly suggest the abandonment of the efforts to treat chronic illness; nor can the nation retreat from pursuing the long-range benefits that may ultimately result from medical research. The Panel suggests, however, that the priority balance within the system should be shifted toward health promotion and disease prevention as major objectives of the nation's health system in the 1980s.

The reduction of suffering and disability, and the saving of human lives, are reasons enough for an increased emphasis on primary prevention. The potential savings because of reduced health care costs provide another reason. The direct costs of treatment, and the indirect costs of the lost earnings, of patients with heart disease and cancer alone are enormous. An estimated 11 percent of the total economic burden of illness in the United States derives from the increased incidence of cancer, heart disease, and other conditions that are associated with smoking—an enormous cost, and one that is partly self-inflicted.

The costs due to smoking are an excellent example of preventable expenditures of health care dollars. The relationship between smoking and illness was highly controversial in 1964 when the first *Surgeon General's Report on Smoking* was published, but the link between smoking and disease is now clearly visible, although the exact medical mechanism is still not understood. From 1973 to 1978 cigarette consumption fell steadily; however, in 1978, one-third of the adult population still smoked. Although the rate for men fell consistently from 1955 to 1978 (from 53 percent to 38 percent), the rate for women rose from 25 percent to 30 percent.[15]

Other risk factors for chronic disease are also potentially preventable. The risk of illness caused by environmental hazards is undoubtedly of enormous magnitude, although concern over this problem has only recently been expressed and the nature and extent of the problem is not certain. Exposure to toxins may be more pervasive than has been believed; more sources of exposure are being located, and more chemical compounds identified as toxic. New sources of environmental hazard to human health, such as nuclear wastes and combustion products from the use of fossil energy sources, are becoming more threatening. And the often subtle actions and interactions of hazards such as pesticides, defoliants, and metallic and organic industrial wastes are coming to be recognized.

Methods for preventing chronic disease will center on the avoidance of exposure to environmental risk factors and life style modification. Alterations in life styles require changes in personal habits that cannot, in most cases, be forced upon the individual.

Public Policy and Disease Prevention

The overriding concern of prevention through life style modification is that the public should not be advised to take action beyond the limits of medical knowledge. Equally important, however, is that health-enhancing behavior be encouraged whenever it is consistent with the state of medical science. There is much that is still unknown in this area, such as the exact relationship between diet and heart disease, the precise impact of secondhand smoke on nonsmokers, and the relationship between exercise and health. Yet more is known than is sometimes admitted. Some relationships are well known and merit immediate action, such as the removal of toxic waste hazards from populated areas or agricultural lands and an active public information program to discourage smoking.

Nutrition and exercise should be advocated in a manner that encourages moderation and prudence. The Assistant Secretary for Health reports that 45 percent of Americans never engage in significant physical activity or exercise, and of the 55 percent who do, most do not meet the minimum time recommendations of medical authorities. Examples of useful policy initiatives include the fluoridation of municipal water supplies, the encouragement of physical fitness programs, and the recommendation of moderation in dietary intake of calories, fat, and salt. Many aspects of the relationships between life style characteristics and health remain obscure, but this should not be used to avoid making recommendations that are known to be helpful. Many of the greatest achievements in disease prevention antedated the understanding of the actual mechanism of the disease process.

Because much of the responsibility for adopting a healthy life style rests with each person, the appropriate governmental role must be largely limited to providing information and incentives so that informed citizens will be able to act responsibly. This information should be accurate and understandable and should reflect a consensus on the behavior that will be most conducive to good health. Current public information materials lack these qualities; they are often confusing, contradictory, and of little or no practical use to the individual or to health care providers.

The government has the opportunity to influence individual life styles. Smoking can be discouraged through the use of antismoking commercials and the prohibition of tobacco advertising. The subsidy to tobacco growers represents a curious conflict of government policies that should now be recognized as contrary to the nation's health. State, local, and federal governments should protect the rights of nonsmokers in public places.

The use of incentives to encourage changes in habits is another tactic available to the government and to the private sector. The health, life, and automobile insurance industries should reward those subscribers who do not smoke and who do wear automobile safety belts. Furthermore, health insurers should be encouraged to reimburse subscribers who stop smoking, practice preventive dentistry, and have regular health appraisals. Employers should discourage employees from smoking and make alcohol rehabilitation and physical fitness programs available.

In the control of environmental hazards, the government's role is more clearly defined. It is generally agreed that the government is responsible for, and perhaps the only body capable of, monitoring and regulating pollutants and hazardous substances in the air, on land, in the water, and in the workplace.

Services associated with disease prevention techniques should be introduced to Medicare and expanded in Medicaid. Further, the early screening of children has never been a comprehensive, universally available program. Such childhood screening and preventive services should be forcefully enacted and monitored.

A suitable vehicle for promoting disease prevention programs at the state level is Public Law 314, which provides block grants to state health departments. The program is weakened by inadequate accountability provisions; these should be remedied through more comprehensive reporting requirements. A new emphasis on health problems associated with particular risk factors, and the simplification and consolidation of the many specified programs (e.g., rat control efforts) is also necessary, as state and local areas will differ markedly in their public health priorities. At present, health departments are often sacrificed to support growing Medicaid programs, so that these public health efforts languish while acute medical care is stressed.

The nation's health care system offers the best care in the world for many diseases. Unfortunately, not all

Americans have shared in its benefits. A great deal of unnecessary disability and many early deaths, especially among disadvantaged groups, can and should be prevented.

The nation's health care system reflects the treatment orientation in every aspect: physician education and training, the organization of services by specialty (often without a primary care provider), and the financing of services. Increased health promotion and disease prevention efforts would improve the longevity of Americans and the quality of their lives. Although many disease prevention questions are not answered, the Panel recommends increased action in these directions during the next decade.

The Elderly

American lives are longer than they were, testimony to a striking success of the medical care system. During the 1980s the quality of this extended life must be made worthy of this success; the elderly must be helped, when necessary, to maintain their dignity.

When illness strikes, elderly people are often badly prepared to deal with the present financial and organizational failings of the health care system. Furthermore, their health and social needs are more complex than those of other population groups. The pattern of health care for the elderly represents in microcosm the deficiencies of the entire health system—in which the focus is curative, not preventive, and problem-oriented, not humanistic.

People 65 years of age and older constitute one of the fastest-growing segments of the nation's population, and the number of elderly people is expected to rise by 20 percent in the 1980s. As a result there will be an increase in the proportion of the population aged 65 and above. In 1978, the more than 23 million elderly persons represented 10.9 percent of the U.S. population. This statistic is expected to reach 12 percent to 13 percent by 1990. Depending on future birth rates, it could be as high as 20 percent within 50 years.

Of greater significance is the changing composition of the elderly population. The group of Americans 75 years of age and older is growing at an even faster rate than is the elderly population as a whole. Because the members of this older group suffer more disabilities than their younger counterparts, they have an even greater need for long-term care.

Surprisingly, the incidence of acute illness among the elderly is lower than that of any other age group. Each episode of illness, however, results in a longer period of convalescence and restricted activity. Medicare was designed to increase elderly persons' access to acute care services and by most criteria it has been successful. However,

49

Medicare does not adequately cover the services needed to ease the effects of chronic, long-term illnesses, although heart disease, cancer, stroke, and many chronic illnesses are most common among the elderly.

Arthritis, senility, and other illnesses associated with the aging process also take a toll of the elderly. These problems manifest themselves as functional limitations that can restrict a person's ability to perform necessary activities of daily life, such as dressing and cooking, or to function in the community, such as making a telephone call or walking to the store. More than one-half of all elderly people suffer from one or more functional limitations that affect their ability to care for themselves, with an even greater percentage of persons aged 75 years and older reporting such limitations. Multiple limitations are common—many elderly people have four or more concurrent functional limitations.

Use of Services

The Panel's concern with the health of the elderly focuses on the long-term care of the frail elderly. Chronic illness must be cared for in a way that maximizes the chances for a return to normal activity and the opportunity to live as dignified and independent a life as possible.

Many elderly people receive care in nursing homes. In fact, 5 percent of the elderly, more than 1.2 million people, currently reside in nursing homes. Furthermore, a person who reaches the age of 65 has a 20 percent to 25 percent chance of entering a nursing home in his or her lifetime. Seventy percent of those who enter a nursing home stay for longer than 1 year; more than half stay for more than 2 years, and many never leave. There is concern not only about the quality of care delivered in nursing homes and the psychological effects of institutionalization, but also about the possibility that many of the people in nursing homes do not really belong there.

An estimated 2 million elderly people with limitations that warrant nursing home care are able to reside in the community. Elderly patients generally prefer community care to a nursing home; it is administered in a less threatening, less regulated environment, and it is less costly.

A Congressional Budget Office study found that between 20 percent and 40 percent of the patients admitted do not really need the intense care provided in a nursing home and could receive adequate care in a community setting.[16] These estimates, which come from surveys comparing the patients' medical needs to the services available in a nursing home, understate the magnitude of the problem. They do not include, for example, patients who enter a nursing home during a phase of an acute illness that could have been prevented if appropriate in-home support services had been available.

An elderly person's ability to remain in the community is a function of the severity of his limitations and the amount of social and personal support available. Such support is generally provided by a spouse or other relative. Nearly 80 percent of elderly persons who require some form of daily assistance and who live in the community are cared for by a relative living in the same household. Such support can often mean the difference between institutionalization and relative independence. Approximately 56 percent of all the elderly, but only 14 percent of the elderly in nursing homes, are married. The highest rates of institutionalization are found in states with the highest rates of emigration of young adults. The lowest rates are observed in populations that stress the importance of the extended family and the role of the elderly in the family network.[17]

Institutional and Home Care

Because of the wide variation in elderly people's needs, both home-based care and institutional care should be available in a community. However, older persons overwhelmingly prefer to remain in their own homes when it is possible. Often a rapid deterioration in an elderly person's physical and mental well-being occurs soon after admission to a nursing home.

The development of a variety of settings providing community-based, noninstitutional care, in addition to home-based services, would well serve people who do not wish to be a burden to their family, do not have family, or who cannot live alone even with social and medical services brought to their homes.

An example of such a concept is "congregate" or "service" housing, which exists in England, in Scandinavia, and, on a much smaller scale, in the United States. Service housing consists of small housing units in buildings that are specially designed for the elderly and the handicapped. Home helpers are assigned to assist the elderly person, and medical and social services are available on call. This type of institution offers an environment in which even a person with serious disabilities can exercise a great degree of independence.

Other types of residential facilities that can provide for the medical and social needs of the elderly under one roof should be examined and discussed. These discussions must consider tradeoffs between the costs of relatively expensive alternatives, such as service housing, and the obvious benefits of these alternatives, measured in terms of the increased morale and satisfaction of the elderly person and in potential savings over the costs of living in a nursing home.

Most families want to care for their elderly, but psychological and physical burdens often prevent them from doing so. If the goal is to allow the elderly person to remain in the community, ways of helping the family to provide for that person's care must be found. One approach is known as respite care; it is occasionally found in the United States, but is much better developed in England. Respite care provides periodic "relief" for the family—the elderly person can be cared for at the respite facility for short periods of time, to allow the family to engage in activities it cannot usually undertake.

Alternatives such as service housing, respite care, and home-based care services have not had the effect on long-term care patterns in the United States that might be expected. This lack of progress in developing alternative care settings and programs stems primarily from the absence of financial backing and incentives to encourage nonmedical services in institutions other than the hospital and the nursing home. Policy analysts note that financing alternative services provides cost savings for those who are able to use less rather than more intensive care, but that these savings are dominated by the costs of care for people who previously did not receive services at all. Whether these additional costs are "worth" incurring depends upon a more careful assessment of utilization patterns and subsequent health effects.

To maximize the ability of the elderly to function independently, they must be able to choose from a variety of living arrangements and services, and both physical and financial access to these facilities and programs must be ensured. Current financing mechanisms have stunted the development of long-term care alternatives, and penalize individuals who may wish to avail themselves of such alternatives.

Financing

Medicare is the major public health insurance program for the elderly, but its capacity to provide financial support for the kinds of services the elderly require is limited. First, its foundations lie in medical care, rather than social care, and they create a bias toward the hospital and the skilled nursing facility as the proper sites of health care delivery. There is little room in such a system for graduated levels of care. Second, Medicare addresses the need for health care in terms of episodes of acute illness, and the needs of the elderly for long-term care of chronic illnesses are continuous in nature. Third, although Medicare covers a substantial number of home health visits, the services provided during these visits and eligibility for these services are highly restricted: the services are strictly medical in nature and must be provided by a qualified nurse or therapist; and they are only provided during an episode of an illness and during the immediate recuperative period. Current Medicare benefits do not encourage the development of graduated, continuous care, and do not provide for the nonmedical services that are needed to keep the elderly person in the community and out of the hospital or nursing home.

There are important questions as to what kinds of alternative care programs should be made available to the elderly, what quantities of homemaker and social services should be provided, and what the eligibility requirements for financial support for these services should be. The Panel nevertheless recommends that the long-term care system emphasize the independent functioning of the elderly and provide services that will allow them the choice of remaining in the community, with family, with friends, or at home for as long as is practical. The Panel notes that there are financial and humanitarian reasons for proceeding with the development of services that broaden the current scope of Medicare within the framework of national health insurance.

1. Health Insurance Institute, *Health and Health Insurance: The Public's View* (Washington, D.C., 1979), p. 26.
2. Congressional Budget Office, *Profile of Health Care Coverage: The Haves and Have-nots* (Washington, D.C., 1979), p. 8.
3. Congressional Budget Office, *Catastrophic Health Insurance* (Washington, D.C., 1977), p. 6.
4. Congressional Budget Office, *Health Differentials Between White and Nonwhite Americans* (Washington, D.C., 1978), p. 5; U.S. Department of Health, Education, and Welfare, *Promoting Health and Preventing Disease: Objectives for the Nation* (Washington, D.C., 1969), p. 62.
5. U.S. Department of Health, Education, and Welfare, Office of the Assistant Secretary for Health, Office of Health Maintenance Organizations, *National Health Maintenance Organization Development Strategy* (Washington, D.C., 1979).
6. M. Freeland, G. Calat, and C. E. Schendler, "Projections of National Health Expenditures, 1980, 1985, and 1990," *Health Care Financing Review* (Winter 1980):1-27; U.S. Department of Health, Education, and Welfare, Office of Research, Statistics, and Technology, *Health: United States* (Washington, D.C., 1979), p. 184. Figures are given in current dollars.
7. E. G. McCarthy and M. L. Finkel, "Second Opinion Elective Surgery Programs: Outcome Status Over Time," *Medical Care* 16:984-994.
8. U.S. Department of Health and Human Services, Office of the Deputy Assistant Secretary for Planning and Evaluation, Health, "Comparison of Effects of Major National Health Insurance Proposals," mimeographed, January 28, 1980.
9. *Ibid.*
10. Congressional Budget Office, Letter from Alice Rivlin, Director, to Senator Edmund Muskie, March 20, 1980.
11. *Health Differentials,* p. 5; J. W. Vaupel, "The Prospects for Saving Lives: A Policy Analysis" (Working paper of the Duke University Center for the Study of Policy Analysis, May 1978), p. 48.
12. "Prospects for Saving Lives," pp. 39-40.
13. *Health: United States,* pp. 117-118.
14. U.S. Department of Health, Education, and Welfare, *Healthy People: The Surgeon General's Report on Health Promotion and Disease Prevention* (Washington, D.C., 1979), pp. 4-5.
15. U.S. Department of Health, Education, and Welfare, *Promoting Health and Preventing Disease: Objectives for the Nation* (Washington, D.C., 1979), p. 78.
16. Congressional Budget Office, *Long-term Care for the Elderly and Disabled* (Washington, D.C., 1979), p. 18.
17. *Ibid.*

Chapter 3

Promoting
THE Welfare
OF AMERICANS IN THE 1980s

The present public welfare system consists of layer upon layer of outdated, sometimes redundant programs. The bureaucratic complexity of the system helps to defeat its object: many persons in need do not receive adequate assistance.

Some of the needs overlooked by the public systems are supplied by private charities and other nonprofit organizations, whose contributions are, and will continue to be, vital to the public good. Nevertheless, the design and implementation of public welfare programs clearly require significant improvement. The Panel is of the opinion that this can best be accomplished by replacing the current maze of programs with a minimum security income.

It cannot be denied that the multiplicity of programs in place today embodies an approach that has not been entirely successful. Poverty persists in America—official estimates placed the number of the poor at 25 million in 1976. This figure comes from Bureau of the Census estimates of how many people have incomes below the official poverty standard. The standard is derived by computing the cost of a "temporary, low budget, nutritious diet" and multiplying that result by a constant chosen to represent the amount of income a family should spend on food. The official poverty standard is modest; in 1978 the poverty level for a typical urban family of four was $6,665.[1]

Some experts dispute the official statistics because the value of such programs as food stamps and Medicaid is not included. By the most optimistic estimates, ones with which this Panel has serious disagreements, 8 million Americans remain poor.

The poor suffer real hardship. Often they do not get enough to eat, and they experience more than their share of sickness. Those poor families that manage to obtain welfare face a harsh existence. An Illinois family on welfare, for example, receives about $500 a month. If $215 is spent for shelter and $149 is used to purchase food, only $136 remains to cover the cost of clothing, household supplies, and everything else. Those who fail to obtain welfare live even more debilitating lives.[2]

The American poor are not randomly distributed. Women account for about two-thirds of the adult poor, and nonwhites are more than twice as likely to be poor as are whites. In fact, almost 16 percent of all nonwhite families were poor in 1976. Government programs do aid nonwhites; but they actually benefit whites more than nonwhites.[3]

The incidence of poverty also varies by region. Recent data show that the South has twice as many poor people as do the North Central states, even after welfare and Social Security benefits are paid.[4]

More disturbing than this persistence of poverty along sexual, racial, and regional lines are recent trends in income levels. Between 1968 and 1972 real income per household rose only 1.7 percent, and the number of families placed in poverty began to increase. Between 1972 and 1976, this trend was exacerbated; real income per household actually dropped 5.0 percent.[5]

It has been argued that the eradication of poverty is an unreasonable goal, one that does not belong on an agenda for the 1980s. The poorest of poor Americans, after all, lives well by world standards. In addition, some analysts think that the nation already spends too much on social welfare, and that the creation of a large welfare establishment has unintentionally erected barriers that prevent people from rising above poverty. The nation, in this view, may have reached the limit of its ability to do good.

The United States does spend a great deal of money for social purposes. Between 1960 and 1975, social welfare expenditures more than quadrupled to $1,319 dollars per capita.* Expenditures that fall more strictly under the heading of welfare have increased at an even greater rate, rising from $34 per capita in 1950 to approximately $187 in 1975. Some $394 billion, a figure equivalent to 19.3 percent of the gross national product (GNP), were spent on social welfare in 1978. In 1965 this share was 11.5 percent.

Social welfare expenditures reached a peak of 20.4 percent of the gross national product in 1975. Their share of the gross national product and of total government spending has declined since 1976. The real rate of growth in social welfare expenditures declined to 2.5 percent by 1979.[6] Because of inflation and other factors that constrain the federal budget, this decline in the growth of social welfare expenditures will probably continue; only a severe recession will arrest the trend.

Poverty and Social Expenditures

---

* The term "social welfare" as used here includes social insurance, public aid, health and medical programs, veterans' programs, education, and housing. Figures are given in current dollars.

The only rationale for the existing welfare system is historical. Each program represents a small piece of history, embodying a politically acceptable approach to a particular problem at the time of the program's creation. There are at least five distinct types of welfare programs, each of which reflects a different approach to aiding the poor or ending poverty. Briefly described, the five types of programs are designed to:

- ☐ Aid members of the "deserving poor;"
- ☐ Define minimum standards;
- ☐ Insure against loss of income;
- ☐ Support the purchase of essentials; and
- ☐ Provide, or promote, opportunity.

Today's system is an uncoordinated collection of past efforts to accomplish not one end, but many.

Aid to the "Deserving Poor"

In the oldest kind of program, the government aids those members of the community who are unable to care for themselves: the very young, the very old, and the disabled. The traditional means of helping such dependent persons was to place them under the care of a family or of the community itself.

In time, institutions such as orphanages and poor farms began to replace this informal system. By 1900, states permitted counties to provide cash grants to the deserving poor. Reliance on local governments to provide aid to the poor ended with the passage of the Social Security Act in 1935, when Congress authorized federal aid to the states for grants to the needy elderly, the blind, and dependent children.

The creation of these federal public assistance categories marked the beginning of what is now called welfare. The basic approach was inherited from the earlier state laws. If a person could show that he was elderly, blind, or a dependent child, and if he could demonstrate need, then he received a cash payment from the local authorities. The federal government paid a portion of the local government's expenses.

With the entry of the federal government into the field of welfare, the informality and flexibility characteristic of local arrangements gave way to rigid categories mandated at the federal level. This approach offered the benefit of what experts call target efficiency—it reached only the poor—but it left gaps in coverage. One had to be more than poor to receive government aid; one had to belong to the "deserving poor," to be old, young, blind, or permanently and totally disabled.

Another type of welfare program, one that defined minimum standards, began during the Progressive Era at the turn of the century. Progressive reformers advocated, and saw passed, protective labor legislation that set minimum standards for working conditions. Typical laws of this kind included child labor laws, maximum hours and minimum wage requirements, safety standards, and workers' compensation laws.

These laws answered perceived needs of the Progressive Era. It should be recalled that women were discouraged from working in those years, and that many Americans were concerned about the disruptions caused by rapid immigration. Conditions differ today. No longer does the nation wish to exclude women or those of foreign origin from the labor force. No longer is there a strict distinction between occupational and nonoccupational problems; no longer does the government limit itself to promulgating social welfare standards, instead taking an active role in maintaining incomes and in protecting people against the risk of sickness. Despite these circumstantial changes, the turn-of-the-century program of minimum standards endures as an American approach to social welfare.

This "standards of decency" approach is beneficial in some respects; however, it has the drawback of sometimes substituting the wish for the deed, particularly in the case of minimum wages. Mandating minimum wages does not ensure that everyone will receive them; it may mean instead that employers choose not to hire those workers whose productivity fails to merit the minimum wage. Ironically, it is the young, the disabled, and the members of minority groups—precisely those whom society seeks to protect through minimum wage legislation—who may suffer by that wage's existence.*

Definition of Minimum Standards

A third type of welfare program, government insurance against loss of income, owes its origin to the passage of the Social Security Act in 1935. The Act created an old-age insurance program; its reach has since been broadened to include survivors' insurance (1939), disability insurance (1956), and health insurance for the elderly (1965). As a result, a program that cost $23.5 million in 1940 now costs $9 billion (in current dollars) and reaches 3.5 million people each month.

Unemployment compensation, or temporary payments to workers laid off from their jobs, also began in 1935 with the passage of the Social Security Act. This program differed from Social Security in that it was run by the

Social Insurance

---

* Among the measures being discussed currently is a differential in the minimum wage applied to youth.

states instead of the federal government. Such program details as which workers were eligible for benefits and the number of weeks they could receive benefits varied greatly from state to state. From a national perspective, the unemployment compensation program, like Social Security, has expanded greatly; the program cost $500 million in 1939 and $17 billion in 1975 (in current dollars).[7]

President Roosevelt, in describing Social Security and unemployment compensation, and federal officials, in administering the programs, took pains not to connect the words "welfare" and "social insurance." Social Security was portrayed as a reliable government insurance program to which all Americans paid premiums and from which all Americans received benefits. These benefits came to people as a matter of right, and the program provided money to rich and poor alike. Programs for the poor, officials believed, made poor programs.

Both Social Security and unemployment insurance, however, contained what could be seen as welfare elements. To deal with the problem of paying everyone adequate benefits, for instance, planners allowed low-wage earners a higher rate of return on their Social Security and unemployment compensation premiums than high-wage earners.

Social Security possessed the additional feature of taking money from workers and giving it to the elderly and disabled. Under the original design of the program, a worker and his employer deposited money in a Social Security account; the worker was to receive it back with interest upon his retirement. In an effort to broaden coverage, raise benefits, and lower payroll taxes, Congress altered the system so that it could be run on a pay-as-you-go basis. After 1939, current workers and their employers paid for the current group of retirees and disabled workers.

The insurance analogy helped to establish Social Security and enabled the program to grow. The very size and success of the program, in turn, produced demands that it do more than insure against loss of income, that it help to deal with some of America's welfare problems. As a public assistance vehicle, however, Social Security was flawed. First, the program failed to reach people outside the labor force who had no income to insure. Second, it developed funding problems that were related to its special feature of relying upon employer and employee contributions. Benefit levels were increased faster than were payroll taxes; this led to occasional shortages in the fund that was used to pay the benefits. (When the postwar generation retires after 2010, this problem will become severe.) Finally, a program built upon the social assumptions of the 1930s contained many outdated elements by the 1980s. Divorced women, for example, received less than did married women.

The intent of a fourth type of government program is to ensure that participants are able to purchase certain essential goods and services, such as food or medical care. Food stamps, for example, may in their modern form be traced to an unsuccessful New Deal experiment and a Kennedy Administration program of 1961.

The food stamp program was extended to the entire nation by Congress in 1964, but it experienced only modest growth until late in the decade.[8] The food stamp program expanded rapidly between 1968 and 1971 for two reasons. First, themes sounded by the Robert Kennedy campaign and by civil rights activists and other reformers made the existence of hunger in an otherwise affluent society unacceptable. Something had to be done to feed the poor quickly, and the food stamp program was conveniently at hand, ready for increased appropriations. Second, members of the Nixon Administration and others who favored simplifying the welfare system saw in food stamps an approach that provided the poor with essentials and could be—in fact, was—administered at the local level. Conservative and liberal members of Congress, able to agree on little else, compromised on the expansion of food stamps. In a series of amendments, benefit levels were increased, uniform eligibility standards were promulgated, and all counties were required to have a program. One authority has called the expansion of food stamps "the most important change in public welfare policy since the passage of the Social Security Act in 1935."[9] The growth of Medicaid, a program that enabled the poor to purchase medical care, matched that of food stamps.

These programs fill real needs, and help to remedy gaps in the American welfare system. Still, these essential purchase programs raise the question of whether the government knows better than the individual what it is good for him to have. Essential purchase aid, in short, owes more to political expediency than to rational planning.

The four classes of welfare programs already discussed involve maintaining the needy. A fifth kind of government aid attempts to raise the poor above poverty by education, rehabilitation, provision of a special social service, or placement in a job.

Welfare programs featuring such government sponsorship of expanded opportunity originated in the 1920s when the benefits of rehabilitation were recognized: instead of allowing a person to become a welfare recipient, he could be trained, counselled, or cured to become a productive citizen. This transformation was doubly attractive, for it contributed to the public as well as the individual good. Among the programs that followed this approach were vocational education and vocational rehabilitation.

These efforts were not meant to include large numbers of people. Each program worked selectively, concentrating on a few clients, and all were run by the casework principle. Vocational rehabilitation, for example, was a painstaking process of direct interviews between a disabled client and a counselor. Each counselor could handle only 75 to 100 cases at any one time; coupled with the small number of counselors, this constraint severely limited the number of people the program could serve. As the counselors were forced to choose among clients, they often selected the most promising clients, those who needed the least help. Rehabilitation programs, therefore, served the mildly impaired and not the severely disabled.

Government efforts to improve opportunity suffered from the fact that they were only as strong as the economy. Almost all of the programs took as their object the eventual placement of their clients into the general labor market. In times of high employment, such as the 1920s, the approach worked relatively well; in hard times the approach almost always failed. These programs, then, failed to deal with the distress caused by recession or depression.

After World War II, an increase in the welfare rolls and an emerging belief that the nation had the means to end poverty prompted a new interest in government promotion of opportunity. The problems of the older programs were forgotten as the nation launched a new series of programs. In 1962, a well-known Congressional supporter spoke of a "realistic program which will pay dividends on every dollar invested. It can move some persons off the assistance rolls entirely, enable others to attain a high degree of self-confidence and independence, encourage children to grow strong in mind and body."[10] Two years later, President Johnson announced the start of the War on Poverty by observing, "We are not content to accept the endless growth of relief rolls or welfare rolls. We want to offer the forgotten fifth of our people opportunity and not doles."[11]

Although the optimism engendered by this hopeful rhetoric faded, a large social service establishment remained. In addition to the programs begun in the 1920s, many states offered a full range of supplementary services, often including day care, family planning, and special transportation programs. In fiscal year 1979, in fact, federal spending for social services amounted to nearly $2.6 billion.[12]

Despite its shortcomings, government promotion of opportunity continues to be a politically attractive means of aiding the poor. Conservative politicians have supported it as an alternative to public assistance, one that is expected to reduce government spending in the long run. Liberal politicians have regarded the stategy as one way of increasing vital social services. Members of both groups like the implicit idea of a permanent solution, through jobs, to the welfare problem.

The most recent example of this type of welfare program is the Comprehensive Employment and Training Act (CETA) of 1974.* This consolidation of federal manpower programs includes social services for adults who are the victims of structural unemployment. In addition, CETA authorizes the Secretary of Labor to provide special services to such groups as native Americans, migrant and seasonal farmworkers, displaced homemakers, the handicapped, persons of limited English-speaking ability, offenders, older workers, and public assistance recipients. Half-buried under layers of confusing regulations and dense jargon, government promotion of opportunity remains an important type of U.S. welfare program.

There are, then, not one but at least five types of government welfare programs. The nation also maintains a large number of private charities, and from an individual's point of view, the result is often confusion. For example, a recently widowed mother of several children, one of whom is disabled, may now apply to seven federal programs for aid. In a typical jurisdiction, she will have to go to at least 4 different offices, fill out at least 5 different forms, and answer some 300 separate questions. The programs may treat the information obtained from these forms differently; the value of the same car, for example, is almost sure to differ from program to program. Fourteen hundred pieces of information may be needed just to determine accurately the level of the woman's income. This illustration underscores the 1974 finding of a Congressional subcommittee:

Inherited Problems

> Instead of forming a coordinated network . . . our . . . income maintenance programs are an assortment of fragmented efforts that distribute income to various persons for various purposes, sometimes on conflicting terms and with unforeseen results.[13]

Despite pleas for simplification, the separate tactics of government aid to the "deserving poor," definition of minimum standards, insurance against loss of income, aid to purchase essentials, and promotion of opportunity all contribute to the present American welfare system. This system is, in effect, a catalogue of historical approaches to social welfare; it features the very oldest as well as the very

---

* The CETA program is discussed in more detail in the report of the Economics Panel.

newest ideas. Attempts to reform the current set of welfare programs must relieve the confusion caused by the persistence of programs long after the time of their enactment.

A Case Study: AFDC

A multiplicity of approaches need not be bad—a diverse population may well require flexibility in bringing welfare to its people. In the United States, however, there is not too much flexibility but too little. The nature of the U.S. political process results in the adoption of outdated approaches to welfare, to solutions that limit the nation's ability to deal with modern problems. The Aid to Families with Dependent Children (AFDC) program is a case in point.

The modern Aid to Families with Dependent Children program began in 1935, but its origins can be found in the early-20th-century widows' pension laws passed by most states. These laws were straightforward in intent. If a widow needed extra money to keep herself and her children at home, the state paid her a pension. Not every widow deserved this sort of aid; she had to be a morally upstanding woman who managed a wholesome home. States conducted vigorous searches for the "gilt-edged" widows who met the qualifications.[14] This process produced what subsequent generations would regard as injustices. In states with large black populations, for example, almost no blacks benefited from widows' pension laws.

With the passage of the Social Security Act, Congress elevated state widows' laws into a federal program of aid to dependent children (later to be called Aid to Families with Dependent Children). At the time, Congress focused its attention on unemployment insurance and old-age assistance; few people, in fact, were interested in aid to dependent children. Control of the program remained largely with the states. They had only to make AFDC available statewide and to meet a few personnel requirements in order to receive federal aid. Passage of AFDC meant, in effect, that federal dollars began to support state widows' pension laws.

After World War II, the public assistance rate began to rise despite high employment levels, and the AFDC program grew faster than all other welfare programs. Other programs limited aid to the elderly, the blind, or the disabled; relatively few people fit these categories. AFDC, however, was available to a much larger population of potential applicants, and this continued to be true during the 1950s.

In 1957, public assistance programs reached a milestone: there were more recipients of AFDC than of any other welfare program. Signs largely unheeded at the time pointed to even greater future growth in AFDC. Poor people were moving from areas with low welfare benefits to areas with high welfare benefits, from the agricultural South to the urban North. If all other factors remained equal, welfare expenditures would rise. In the 1960s, too, many young people would themselves have children and create a larger pool of potential welfare applicants.

By the late 1950s and early 1960s the AFDC program assisted families of deserted mothers and children, and of mothers and illegitimate children, as well as widows and orphans. A study commissioned by the Eisenhower Administration recognized this in 1960, stating that AFDC made financial assistance available for the protection and care of 2.3 million "homeless, dependent, and neglected children . . . found not only where a parent is dead or physically incapacitated, but also in families where there is desertion, divorce, or, indeed, where there was no marriage."[15]

With the realization that the nature of the AFDC caseload had changed came a new concern over the breakdown of the family and community structures. Thoughtful individuals realized that the AFDC program did little to deal with family or community breakdown—if anything, the law encouraged families to separate. A larger group of the poor found that a mother and father living separately could do better financially than could a family living together. If the parents were separated, AFCD allowed the parent with the child to collect welfare; the family that lived together had less access to public aid.

One solution to this difficulty was to redesign the welfare system to permit the federal government to aid all poor people. This idea had existed for a long time in the form of a proposal for a federally aided general assistance program, but political considerations forced program officials to set the idea aside. New domestic programs, particularly new social welfare programs, proved difficult to create in the postwar years; only in the early New Deal and Great Society periods did a strong consensus on the need for new efforts exist.

Although expansion in the welfare rolls alarmed Americans, they still regarded welfare as primarily a local responsibility and as a means to aid the "deserving poor." Nonetheless, there were two significant reforms in the AFDC program during the Kennedy Administration. In 1961 the program was amended to add a provision for unemployed parents. The next year Congress passed a measure that added rehabilitation services to AFDC.

The unemployed parent provision revealed some of the weaknesses in the combined federal-state approach to public welfare. Instead of limiting AFDC to one-parent families, coverage was extended to two-parent families, provided that the primary wage earner was unemployed. States were not required to participate in this part of the

AFDC program, however, and half of them did not. Those states that did extend their AFDC program were the ones with relatively high welfare benefits.

The unemployed parent provision was closely linked to traditional patterns of helping the poor. Requirements for participation were stringent. To qualify the family for aid, one of the parents had to be unemployed; to be certified as unemployed, the primary wage earner must have worked 6 of the 13 calendar quarters prior to his application for welfare. Once on welfare, he was forbidden to work more than 100 hours a month. Because many states failed to participate in the extended program and because it contained this work restriction, enrollment remained low. In 1979, for example, 3.5 million one-parent families and only 120,000 two-parent families received AFDC.[16]

The 1962 amendments emphasized the rehabilitation of welfare recipients; they authorized federal reimbursement for 75 percent of the costs of rehabilitative and preventive services. It was thought that this would make welfare recipients more independent and self-reliant, and prevent the development of a "culture of poverty." If the aim of the program was to lower the number of families receiving AFDC, it failed. Social services proved a poor match for the demographic forces that were creating a larger population of potential welfare applicants. In addition, these social services worked selectively; they were not available to all welfare recipients.

In 1967 a new attempt to deal with the AFDC problem, the Work Incentive Program (WIN), appeared. This represented an explicit effort to place welfare recipients in the labor market. Under WIN, all able-bodied adults receiving AFDC benefits were given the opportunity to acquire vocational skills and work experience. However, WIN failed to lower the number of people on welfare caseloads; in the program's first 4 years, AFDC rolls increased by 3 million people. Congress responded with the Talmadge amendments in 1971: all able-bodied AFDC recipients without responsibilities for children under 6 were required to register for WIN services, and program administrators were required to spend one-third of their budgets on subsidized training and employment.

Here was a notable irony: the AFDC program, created explicitly to keep mothers at home with their children, and out of the labor force, was now being asked to do exactly the opposite. This was the result of a political dynamic that enabled existing programs to be amended but prevented new programs from being passed.

AFDC became the nation's principal public assistance program. As a program in aid of the "deserving poor," it worked well. As the nation's major means-tested program, which AFDC had become by default, it was not a success.

In such a means-tested program, aiding one-parent families and keeping mothers out of the labor force were not desirable. The development of AFDC illustrated how old programs failed to conform to new conditions.

Many of the problems of AFDC and the other programs of the U.S. social welfare system concern the three goals of a modern welfare system—equity, adequacy, and efficiency. Ideally, the nation's welfare programs should treat similar people in a similar manner, the concept of equity. It should provide benefits that give all households an income above the poverty level, the goal of adequacy, and it should contain incentives to substitute work for welfare wherever possible, the target of efficiency. The present system meets none of these criteria.

Adequacy, Equity, Efficiency

The system fails to meet the goal of equity in part because the programs classify people according to the original "deserving poor" categories. As a Congressional subcommittee noted, "with few exceptions, people are only more or less employable, not employable or unemployable."[17] This modern truth suggests that the "deserving poor" approach to welfare creates fundamental inequities. An able-bodied person of working age who has neither children nor job skills can be poor; so can a 59-year-old man whose health is breaking down. Neither of these people qualifies for federal assistance, but others in similar circumstances, who have children or are a few years older, do qualify.

Sometimes the requirements of the programs produce social pathologies that compound the system's inequities. To use a pointed example, a Minnesota mother of three could receive AFDC, Medicaid, and food stamps until her income reached $8,000 a year. A Minnesota father who remained with his family and worked full-time at a low wage disqualified his family for aid, regardless of need. In 1972, according to a Congressional subcommittee, a man who worked for $2.00 an hour could increase the annual income of his family (a wife and two children) by an average of $2,158 if he deserted them.[18] The system in these cases rewarded one family over another, and many would argue that it rewarded the wrong family.

Because welfare benefits cannot be given to everyone, an income level beyond which aid is terminated is established. This threshold, or notch, produces inequities. If a person who earns $19 is entitled to Medicaid, but someone who earns $20 is not, severe problems result. By making $1 less, the first person gains benefits worth a great deal; he begins by making less money and ends by having the use of more money than the second person. The second person may decide that he will be better off if he works less. A welfare system with sharp notches, therefore, produces inefficiencies as well as inequities.

The persistence of poverty testifies to the fact that the goal of adequate benefits is not being met. Some people who qualify for benefits fail to receive them; others live in the 24 states where benefits from AFDC and food stamps amounted to less than three-quarters of the poverty line in 1977. Still others reside in states with comparatively high welfare benefits that have not been adjusted for inflation and have consequently become less than adequate.

The welfare system fails to meet the goals of adequacy, equity, and efficiency. Once programs are in place they tend to stay in place, long after the conditions that created them, and the needs to which they should respond, have changed. These observations argue for the need to create a coherent welfare system.

A Systematic Approach

The events of the past 20 years may be seen as the maturing of the social welfare system. In a mature system, coverage ceases to be limited to a small and select group; a far greater percentage of the poor benefits from social programs. Work incentives become important as programs reach beyond the "deserving poor" and begin to affect labor force participants. Receipt of multiple benefits becomes more common. By these criteria, the social welfare programs of the past 20 years have begun to function systematically. This tendency would be far greater if the interactions and common effects of programs were carefully considered during the planning process.

A number of schemes for such reform of the system have recently received public attention. Many plans rely upon the idea of a negative income tax, an idea that followed from the observation that welfare programs penalize work. If a person who earns a dollar loses a dollar in welfare benefits, he has little incentive to work, because there is, in effect, a tax of 100 percent on his earnings. To remedy the problem, he must be allowed to keep a certain percentage of his earnings. In fact, federal officials have long tried to create work incentives within individual programs, but the results of these experiments have been unsatisfactory.

The Negative Income Tax

If a universal negative income tax were adopted, all families would receive the guarantee of a minimum cash benefit and pay a tax of less than 100 percent on earnings. Suppose there were a guaranteed benefit of $2,000 and a 50 percent tax rate on earnings. A family with no earnings would receive the guarantee of $2,000 from the government. A family that earned $2,000 would receive the guarantee and keep half of its earnings; the guarantee of $2,000 and the after-tax

67

earnings of $1,000 total $3,000, so the government would give $1,000 to this family. A family that earned $4,000 would receive the guarantee and retain $2,000 in earnings, for a total of $4,000; this family would neither receive money from the government nor owe the government money.

In the 1970s the negative income tax moved from the realm of idea to the status of a serious Congressional proposal with the introduction of the Nixon Administration's Family Assistance Plan (FAP). The Family Assistance Plan contained a proposal to provide a federal minimum cash payment to all families with dependent children; the AFDC program would have been eliminated. The bill containing the Family Assistance Plan was not passed, but it was followed by a series of proposals that used the negative income tax idea. In 1974 the Income Supplement Program proposal appeared; this was a negative income tax scheme that would have replaced food stamps, AFDC, and welfare programs for the elderly and disabled. Later in the decade, the Joint Economic Committee's Subcommittee on Fiscal Policy recommended a negative income tax after 3 years of study.[19]

Although the negative income tax failed to gain Congressional passage, those programs that were created followed the general principles of a negative income tax. Amendments to the food stamp program transformed it into a guaranteed income, payable in food stamps, and Supplemental Security Income created a guaranteed annual income for the elderly and the disabled. Administrative control over the traditional welfare categories (the aged, the blind, and the disabled) was transferred from the states to the federal government. In 1974, when the Supplemental Security Income program went into effect, an estimated 6.2 million Americans were eligible for benefits.

The liberalization of food stamps and creation of Supplemental Security Income exemplified a creative blend of new ideas and old traditions. These programs follow two of the traditional American approaches to welfare, aid to the "deserving poor" and aid to purchase essentials; at the same time, they incorporate new ideas about work incentives and efficient administration associated with negative income tax schemes.

The more ambitious aspects of the negative income tax proposals, such as a guaranteed income for the working poor, failed partly because they demanded sacrifices from groups that fare relatively well under existing programs, such as the veterans of foreign wars and the blind. Welfare programs that accommodate such special interests retained their appeal because they concentrated benefits upon a

Obstacles to Comprehensive Reform

readily identifiable group, a seemingly sensible tactic in a small welfare system. Under modern conditions, this practice blocks systematic reform by creating groups that have nothing to gain from such reform.

The negative income tax proposals also failed because legislators had few opportunities to acquire a comprehensive view of the social welfare system. Committee structures helped to lock legislators into a program-by-program view of social policy. Control over income maintenance, for example, was divided among more than 60 Congressional committees and subcommittees in 1980.[20] This circumstance helped to reinforce legislators' natural loyalties to programs they had helped to design or to pass, loyalties that are abandoned only reluctantly.

More than political and structural considerations prevented the passage of a negative income tax; there were also serious questions related to cost. Locked within the arithmetic were difficult social choices. Providing adequate benefits just for the poor requires setting high tax rates on additional income earned by the poor (the marginal tax rate). On the other hand, these high tax rates discourage people from working.

If the marginal tax rate were lowered, the income level at which the government would continue to pay benefits would rise. Halving the tax rate doubles this break-even point, and doubling the break-even point would bring welfare payments to many families not considered poor. Congress showed great reluctance to take this action. In addition, if benefits were available at the income levels earned by the greatest number of families, the number of families on welfare and the costs of welfare programs would both increase greatly.

Results from social experiments suggested potential problems. Attempts to simulate the effects of a negative income tax in Seattle and Denver led to the finding that the negative income tax decreased the number of hours worked, particularly by wives in two-parent families. This phenomenon was the result, in part, of broadening welfare coverage to some groups who were previously excluded. Secure in their new income, some people chose to reduce the number of hours they worked.[21]

Acceptance of the principles of the negative income tax was nevertheless common among welfare reformers by the end of the 1970s. There was widespread agreement that welfare coverage should be expanded, benefits made more equitable, and work incentives improved. The expansion of the food stamps program and the passage of Supplemental Security Income indicated wider acceptance of the tenets, if not all the implications, of a negative income tax.

By the late 1970s, a new approach to large-scale reform of the welfare system emerged: the concept of a guaranteed job. The poor were to be divided into two groups, one of which was expected to work. Mothers of dependent children, the disabled, and the elderly were not expected to work; they would receive a relatively high guaranteed income. Those who were expected to work would receive a lower guarantee and the opportunity to raise themselves above poverty by means of a guaranteed job. Some of the proposals, such as the Carter Administration's Program for Better Jobs and Income, included an 8-week screening period during which the applicant would receive help in looking for a job in the private sector. If he were unable to find one, the applicant would be given either a public service job or a government-subsidized job with a private employer. One source of such employment would be an expanded CETA program.

Although this new idea has much to recommend it, it also presents problems and uncertainties. No one knows if the nation has the ability to find or create jobs for all who want to work. More than a million new jobs may be required, a substantial number of which would be in the public sector. During a severe recession, the numbers of jobs needed would rise, and these jobs may cost the government more than cash payments would. Special social services for mothers of children older than 6, such as after-school programs, may have to be offered, and these services are costly. In addition, no one knows if the recipients would remain in these jobs, move on to private employment, or, indeed, come to work. Wage levels will play a crucial role in this respect. Wages, which cannot be set lower than the minimum wage, may draw many people out of private-sector jobs.

Finally, there remains the vexing problem of separating those who are expected to work from those who are not expected to work. Simple guidelines may apply to families with dependent children, but defining who is disabled has always been difficult. Disability programs have experienced great growth partly because no objective criteria for defining "disability" exist. Often programs rely on impairments, such as the loss of a limb, as the criteria by which to make judgments, and may unfairly relegate many productive people to the disabled category.

Some have urged the creation of a means-tested general assistance program under which any person who could demonstrate poverty would receive a flat payment. This approach, explored in various forms by conservative thinkers since the 1950s, has the virtues of directing aid to the poor and reducing total expenditures.

Guaranteed Jobs

General Assistance

70

The most recent such proposal would provide federal block grants to the states for the purpose of making welfare payments. Each state would receive the same amount of money that it presently receives for AFDC. States would then be responsible for any cost increases and for any expansions of the program they chose to undertake, and would retain any savings that they were able to effect.[22]

Because these plans depend on a caseworker's services, they are frequently both costly and inefficient. The block grant proposal will also perpetuate the disparities that exist in the levels of state welfare payments. States with low benefits would continue to pay low benefits; in fact, they would be rewarded for providing low benefits.

In summary, then, a number of welfare reform proposals have appeared in the past decade. The negative income tax would eliminate some existing programs, substituting an income guarantee and a tax on earnings that would supply incentives to work. Another, the work-and-welfare proposal, would attempt to substitute work and wages for government cash payments. Still another would broaden coverage under a traditional public assistance format. All of these proposals involve thinking about welfare as a comprehensive system rather than as a collection of scattered programs.

Conclusion

At this point the discussion of welfare should be summarized and some conclusions drawn.

Poverty persists in America despite a large array of welfare programs that take at least five distinct approaches to the problem. The system itself consists of layer upon layer of programs. These programs are difficult to enact; they tend to remain in place for a long time, resulting in a system with too many programs that nonetheless leaves many people in need without adequate help.

Changed conditions in the 1980s will make the need for system reform more urgent. The median age of the population will continue to rise, and public attention will shift from the problems of dependent children to those faced by the elderly. In all likelihood, the pressures on the social budget will become more severe. Inflation will continue to affect the economy, and the poor, adversely. Without substantial reform, the welfare system will simply become more of an anachronism, more out of touch with modern problems and needs.

The Panel believes that many types of programs (such as those that set minimum standards, offer aid to purchase essentials, and help the "deserving poor") are no longer as important as they once were. Now the system must work toward providing all Americans, and particularly those

Americans with incomes below the poverty line, with a modicum of security.

Income maintenance therefore must take precedence over other welfare goals, even such important goals as employment training and aid to the disadvantaged. The Panel believes that it should be the national policy to seek an end to poverty through the provision of a minimum security income for all Americans, and that this should be affirmed through legislation.

In placing paramount importance on the goal of income maintenance, the Panel does not mean to slight the problems of civil rights, health care, and education. Each of these concerns is addressed elsewhere in this report. This recommendation is based on a simple observation: of all the things the poor desire, they want money most of all, for money enables them to purchase health care, education, and other social services.

Furthermore, testimony before this Commission and other evidence suggest convincingly that income maintenance is a proper function of the federal government. The experience of the 1970s bears out this judgment. Under the rubric of the New Federalism, efforts were made to strengthen local decisionmaking. In the process of sorting out the government's functions, however, the proponents of the New Federalism decided that programs that transferred money from the government to individuals should be administered by the federal government. The Panel agrees with this assessment.

Local governments, for their part, have an important role to play in the provision of social services. People who live in troubled communities know the problems of those communities best, and they deserve a say in how the community deploys its resources to solve those problems. Local governments and private, nonprofit, voluntary charities have worked together closely in the past; the government's provision of a minimum income will free private charity to do its beneficent work.

The private sector must also be prepared to accept responsibility if the nation is to reach its goal of providing a minimum security income for all Americans. Jobs in the private marketplace are the best solution to the problems of welfare. It remains for the government only to secure the essentials of life to its citizens.

The Panel therefore favors the creation of a minimum security income with a guarantee set initially at three-quarters of the poverty line and a 50 percent tax on earnings. This new program would replace Aid to Families with Dependent Children, food stamps, and the general assistance programs. The Supplemental Security Income program would make additional grants to the elderly and disabled in order to bring the income of those groups up to the poverty line.

Many of the objections to this plan will concern its cost. In all likelihood, welfare costs would rise, at least in the first years of the plan. The plan would raise benefit levels in many states, and it would expand welfare coverage. Estimates prepared for this Commission place the additional cost of the minimum security income program to the federal government at $15 billion to $20 billion.[23]

Although the plan would cost a great deal, its advantages outweigh its disadvantages. The plan would end many of the problems created by an incremental approach to welfare and ensure that the welfare system functioned coherently. No longer would the state of Alabama pay an average of $37 to each welfare recipient and the state of Hawaii pay an average of $115, a difference far in excess of the relative costs of living. The plan would establish an incentive for those on welfare to work by lowering the tax on their earnings. It would end the incentive for poor families to separate, and it would go far toward eliminating the burden that the welfare system now places on women.

The plan also offers the government many potential savings. Significant reform of Social Security could occur. States could devote more of their budgets to social services, for they would no longer carry the burden of paying a share of AFDC costs as well as the entire cost of general assistance. In fact, the welfare system could be cleared of much of its clutter and confusion, and private charities could play an expanded role. All of these developments would produce cost savings.

Commissioner Juanita Kreps recently expressed the Panel's views on welfare reform in an eloquent manner. "Eliminating poverty is affordable," she said. "What we cannot afford is its persistent devastation of the human spirit." Twenty years after the beginning of the War on Poverty, the insight remains timely.

1. U.S. Department of Commerce, Bureau of the Census, *Current Population Reports,* series P-60, no. 115 (Washington, D.C., 1978), p. 15.
2. President's Commission for a National Agenda for the Eighties, Hearings in Chicago, Ill., July 22, 1980, transcript. Testimony of the Public Welfare Coalition for a Humane Public Aid Program in Illinois.
3. Diane Pearce, "The Feminization of Poverty: Women, Work, and Welfare," *Urban and Social Review* 11:28-36; U.S. Commission on Civil Rights, *Social Indicators of Equality for Minorities and Women* (Washington, D.C., 1978), pp. 47-67; Congressional Budget Office, *Poverty Status of Families Under Alternative Definitions of Income,* Background Paper 19 (Washington, D.C., 1977).
4. *Poverty Status,* p. 16.
5. Sheldon Danziger and Robert Plotnick, "Has the War on Poverty Been Won?" Paper delivered at the Second Annual Middlebury College Conference on Economic Issues, Middlebury, Vt., April 1980.
6. U.S. Department of Health and Human Services, Social Security Administration, Office of Research and Statistics, "Social Welfare Expenditures, Fiscal Year 1978," research and statistics note (Washington, D.C., 1980).
7. Daniel S. Hamermesh, *Jobless Pay and the Economy* (Baltimore, Md. 1977); U.S. Department of Health, Education, and Welfare, Social Security Administration, Office of Research and Statistics, "Monthly Benefit Statistics" (Washington, D.C., 1979).
8. Maurice McDonald, *Food Stamps and Income Maintenance* (New York, 1973).
9. President's Commission, Hearings, testimony of Richard Nathan.
10. Senator Ribicoff, as quoted in Gilbert Steiner, *Social Insecurity: The Politics of Welfare* (Chicago, 1966), p. 39. The Senator is referring to the Public Welfare Amendments of 1962.
11. Lyndon B. Johnson, "Remarks upon Signing the Economic Opportunity Act, August 20, 1964," *Public Papers of the Presidents 1963-64* (Washington, D.C., 1965), 2:988.
12. U.S. Congress, General Accounting Office, "U.S. Income Security System Needs Leadership, Policy, and Effective Management" (Washington, D.C., 1980), p. 22.
13. U.S. Congress, Joint Economic Committee, Subcommittee on Fiscal Policy, "Income Security for Americans: Recommendations of the Public Welfare Study" (Washington, D.C., 1974).
14. Roy Lubove, *The Struggle for Social Security* (Cambridge, Mass., 1968).
15. President's Commission on National Goals, *Goals for Americans* (Englewood Cliffs, N.J., 1960), p. 257.
16. James R. Hosek, "The AFDC-Unemployed Fathers Program: Determinants of Participation and Implications for Welfare Reform" Paper delivered at the Second Annual Middlebury College Conference on Economic Issues, Middlebury, Vt., April 1980.
17. "Income Security for Americans."
18. *Ibid.*
19. *Ibid.*
20. President's Commission, Hearings, testimony of Senator Durenberger; "U.S. Income Security System Needs Leadership, Policy, and Effective Management."
21. U.S. Department of Health, Education, and Welfare, *Summary Report: Seattle, Denver Income Maintenance Experiment* (Washington, D.C., 1978).
22. Robert B. Carleson, "The Alternatives: True Reform or Federalization," *Commonsense* 3:13-23.
23. Cost estimates were prepared for the Commission by the Urban Institute.

Chapter 4

Education
AN

AGENDA FOR THE 1980s

I n the 1980s, there must be a new, firm commitment
to the quality and vitality of public education.
Many think that economic conditions will force a
reduced effort in this field; but such lowered expectations reflect a possibly dangerous order of priority.
Public education is crucial to the survival and future of
American democracy.

It is the belief of the Panel that the students of the
1980s must be offered equality of educational opportunity,
competence of instruction, and the chance to develop their
individual talents to the full. These three—equality, competence, and excellence—are the essential items on the national education agenda. A continued commitment to
equal access to learning opportunities is of critical importance, and it must be accomplished in a way that improves
the overall quality of public schools. Barriers to a satisfac-
tory education for the nation's students—barriers of
poverty, prejudice, and indifference—must be removed.

Public schools in the United States have long carried a
dual responsibility, to the community and to the individual. They have served the community by providing
the education necessary for effective social, economic, and
political participation in the democracy, and by transmit-
ting social values and beliefs to new generations. At the
same time, the availability of public education, including
higher education, has offered the individual the opportunity for intellectual growth and self-fulfillment. In return,
the school system has received a measure of public support
normally tendered only the most revered institutions.

It is commonplace, but nonetheless true, that the
changes in American society of the past 20 years have
moved more rapidly and visibly than those of earlier years.
Hardly any aspect of American life, from the structure of
the family to the form and activities of corporations, remains unaltered. Inevitably, in these circumstances, the
public schools have failed to meet public expectations.
These expectations have not always been consistent with
one another. The public appears to believe that schools can
solve society's problems, without sufficiently acknowl-

edging the extent to which these same problems have beset the schools.

The public school system is perhaps the most sensitive of civic institutions. It is immediate—most people's children attend public schools—and it is, in a way, the real focus of people's hopes. However, many young people have come to feel alienated from society, from family, school, business, and to doubt that the American dream of success is attainable. It is commonly accepted, and perhaps increasingly true, that social advancement is impossible without education. The Panel believes that the essential mission of the school is to give students the basic skills and social experience required to become functional and productive citizens in a democratic society. To achieve this goal, public schools must receive the support of the community at large—and school personnel must be accountable for the students' proficiency in the basic skills.

Among the changes of the past two decades is an increased awareness of the special needs of some groups and of the changing needs of others. Economically and educationally disadvantaged students have been enrolled in unprecedented numbers. Recent federal legislation has made it possible for an increasing number of physically, emotionally, and mentally handicapped students and students of limited English fluency to enter the public schools. These children have required particular forms of assistance and special skills of the schools, and the schools have not always been able to provide them. Other needs—such as the need for new vocational programs designed to respond to the transformation of the electronics industry—were met with varying success.

The schools' efforts to adjust to expanded responsibilities have been watched closely—by parents, by federal administrators, by special-interest advocates, by teachers' unions, by the courts, and by the press. The influence of these groups came to be increasingly felt. Public schools have been under great pressure from the courts and the federal government to respond quickly and effectively to situations for which they were unprepared or which they were unwilling to accept. Teachers' unions challenged the school system's authority in order to provide their members with needed compensation and improved working conditions, but teachers' strikes also weakened the public's traditional respect for the profession.

Whatever the actual success of the schools in responding to a complex variety of pressing demands, the public reaction to the schools' response has been critical, and the criticism has often been expressed with acerbity. Concern for the quality of the education offered in the public schools has been sharpened by lowered scores on tests of basic skills and scholastic aptitude (required by many colleges as part of the admission procedure). Some parents began to doubt that the public schools were offering their children the education that they deserved. Educators believe that the combined effect of these factors, and of others unspecified here, is that the supporters of public education have lost a clear sense of common purpose at the same time that the responsibilities of the system have been enlarged and extended. The public schools are being asked to perform their traditional role more effectively and efficiently and also to develop effectual responses to an additional set of educational needs, needs that will have considerable impact upon American society in the 1980s.

The school system will be called upon to provide a quality, integrated education; to satisfy a widening insistence on equity in educational opportunities; to offer greater diversity and choice and to maintain higher standards; to respond to demands for accountability; and to meet society's requirements for educated, skilled workers in new fields. A rapidly expanding technology, especially in the processing and transmittal of information, must be accommodated. The present focus on classroom instruction must be changed to a broader involvement with learning resources to be found outside the schools. Educators will have to direct and develop educational institutions in ways that create self-renewal mechanisms for those institutions and the individuals who serve in them.

The current crisis of confidence in public schooling is more widespread, persistent, and intense than ever before. This is precisely the time to reaffirm the legacy and potential of public education. A commitment to excellence in public education for children of all abilities is fundamental to the American ideal of a just society.

The Challenge: Constructive Confidence

The Panel believes that the nation has the will and the creativity to restore confidence and quality in the public schools. There are many examples of successful renewal, of significant improvements that confirm that quality in education can be achieved. A practical support of this effort is public consideration of those functions that the schools can reasonably and effectively perform. It is commonly agreed that schools should give children basic skills and knowledge; should they also offer instruction in foreign languages and the arts? Provide psychological counseling and vocational training? Socialize children to the core values of society? And how—by the expenditure of which monies, by the use of which methods of teaching and discipline—are the schools to accomplish these tasks?

The public school offers an appropriate focus for the discussion of some of the fundamental dichotomies of American society: equity and excellence; homogeneity and pluralism; competition and cooperation; individuality and community; investment and consumption. Conflicting opinions about the role of the public school, if any, in teaching values, sex education, work habits, and citizenship should also be addressed.

The importance of public debate on these matters leads some Panel members to recommend that public education forums be held in every state. Separate meetings could be held in various localities, perhaps sponsored by the county governments, and could culminate in a state conference of local delegates. By this means, the residents of the nation's 16,000 school districts—the people who make the critical local decisions about public schools— might be afforded an opportunity to recognize and discuss the consequences of their decisions.

The present atmosphere of critical dissidence, of discrete values and needs advanced by separate groups, may be helped to resolution through the opportunity to discuss common interests as well as special needs. Furthermore, this greater local participation in debating, defining, and setting national goals is of crucial importance. It draws upon the nation's greatest strength—the experience, knowledge, and concern of its citizens—and focuses that strength upon one of the nation's greatest challenges.

Other Panel members, including the Chairman, question the utility of such forums. They worry that such meetings will create the illusion of progress and lead only to cosmetic solutions to educational problems. These Commissioners believe strongly in the importance of local participation in the solution to social problems, but they also feel that the proposed education forums would cause attention and concern to shift from the schools themselves to the communities in which the schools are situated.

Some of the issues now under public discussion—desegregation, compensatory education programs, school finances, and the role of standardized tests, to name several—have been addressed for years. The failure to resolve them points to their complexity and does not lessen their importance.

The Major Issues

The federal government has been, and will be, substantially involved with educational matters by virtue of its responsibility for matters affecting civil rights and the commerce of the nation. Federal funds for research, technological development, and the training of scholars help to support the activities of public and private institutions. Clearly, there is a continuing and significant federal role in public education policy.

Background

78

The current federal role in education is designed to ensure equal educational opportunity and to provide special forms of support to certain groups; to implement judicial decisions; to strengthen state and local efforts in meeting educational needs; to promote the quality of education through research, evaluation, and information sharing; and to improve the coordination, management, and accountability of federal programs. The federal presence in education has grown from a few programs ($950 million in 1960) to more than 100 programs ($11.6 billion in 1978); still the federal share of total school expenditures is only 9 percent.[1] The depth of Congressional concern about the limits of this role is evidenced by the fact that there are more federal laws regulating education than any other activity. Furthermore, Congress has directed that the Department of Education shall not increase the authority of the federal government over education or diminish the responsibilities that are reserved to the states.

Federal funds are accompanied by many regulations governing their use: requirements for the separate accounting of funds and the segregation of federal expenditures; procedures for federal participation in decisions affecting fund allocations; definitions of children eligible to participate in federally sponsored programs; requirements for parent and community advisory groups; and requirements for the regular submission of data. Compliance with these regulations can be both expensive and time-consuming. These and other aspects of categorical aid programs will remain on the education agenda in the 1980s.

A strong attachment remains throughout this nation to state, local, and private control of education, and to the retention of a structural and programmatic diversity that responds to widely varying interests. The federal government does not have primary responsibility in the field of public education; the willingness of state governments and local school districts to administer programs effectively is the key to success of federal programs. The basic curriculum and other educational matters specifically not legislated by Congress remain within the province of state and local governments. To fulfill their responsibilities, state and local governments carry 47 percent and 44 percent, respectively, of total school expenditures.[2]

Desegregation. The principal federal responsibility in education followed from the enforcement of civil rights legislation. During the 1950s and 1960s, the focus of school desegregation efforts was on the Southern states that had specific laws requiring separate schools for blacks and whites. In the 1970s, antidiscrimination efforts were broadened to include Northern and Western schools that

**Equal
Educational
Opportunity:
Special Needs**

have been segregated by a combination of private and public actions. The legal determination of what constitutes discrimination in such circumstances and what constitutes an adequate remedy has been more difficult to make and easier to challenge than it had been in the South.

The federal courts, while remaining faithful to enforcing the principles of *Brown* v. *Board of Education*,[3] have also been guided by the U.S. Supreme Court's continued reliance on an "intent" standard for imposing a duty to desegregate a public school system. This reliance makes no allowance for the fact that schools segregated by circumstances may be as harmful to children as are schools segregated by law.

There are now more than 300 court-ordered desegregation plans in effect, and more litigation is probable. More, not less, concerted action is needed on the part of the federal government, the courts, and the states to implement the letter and spirit of the *Brown* decision. The Panel recommends active federal support for methods of achieving quality integrated education such as redistricting, pairing of schools, and court-approved transportation plans. Other avenues should also be explored.

The transportation of students has received an inordinate amount of attention, although it is only one of a number of techniques for desegregating schools. In 1978, 50 percent of 42 million public elementary and secondary school children were bused to school; less than 3 percent of such transportation was for the purpose of school desegregation.[4] In the 1980s, if the school system is to be racially integrated, there should be a reassessment of the current prohibition of a city-suburban interdistrict remedy to segregated schools.[5] Where present school district lines are barriers to equal educational opportunity and integrated schooling, they will have to be redrawn. Further, desegregation must be supported by providing teachers and administrators with adequate training in the curriculum, social, and organizational changes that usually accompany desegregation.

A fundamental reality of the 1980s is that the racial imbalance of the cities is growing. A real solution to the problem of segregated schools would require comprehensive, coordinated government programs in housing, transportation, commerce, education, and criminal justice. More effective federal policies and actions in these fields are feasible; the Department of Justice, for example, recently reorganized its Civil Rights Division in order to coordinate housing and education litigation. However, the costs of racial isolation will mount as the implementation of desegregation plans is delayed.

Economically and Educationally Disadvantaged Students. Title I of the Elementary and Secondary Education Act of 1965 provides funds for compensatory education services for students of low achievement in school districts where there are many students from low-income families. In 1980, 5 million children (11.6 percent of total school enrollment) participated in this program; the cost was $3.5 billion. An estimated 3 million children need, but are not now receiving, such compensatory education services, and some children who are now participating could be served longer and better.[6] Positive Title I program evaluation studies persuade this Panel to recommend increased Title I funding for economically and educationally disadvantaged elementary school students in the 1980s.

Basic skills test scores of disadvantaged students in the 7th through the 12th grades have shown little or no improvement during the past decade. Compensatory education services for educationally and economically disadvantaged students in secondary schools are essential, and at present there are very few programs designed for this purpose. Policy decisions in the future should address the choice between increasing funding and redistributing existing funds. The roles of federal, state, and local governments in supporting compensatory education in secondary schools should be reconsidered.

Another equal educational opportunity concern is the prevention of discrimination against female students. Enforcement of Title IX of the Education Amendments of 1972 is an important means of achieving educational equity for women. In addition to Title IX enforcement, federally supported counseling programs can be used to encourage female students to pursue careers in science and technology, to enroll in traditionally "male" courses, and to participate in athletic programs. Federal and state grants could be used to study sex-role stereotyping in textbooks and other problems unique to female students.

Handicapped Students. A 1975 federal statute, Public Law 94-142, requires a "free appropriate public education" in the least restrictive environment for all emotionally, mentally, or physically disabled children 3 to 21 years old. In 1978 and 1979, almost 4 million children were served under the provisions of this law at a cost of $850 million. Estimates of as yet unserved handicapped children range from 2 to 5 million.[7]

State support of special education for the handicapped is now the largest and most rapidly growing element of state categorical financial assistance to local schools. This growth (14.3 percent annually since 1975) is likely to continue as more local school districts face financial problems.[8] Additional funds are, and will be, needed.

A source of some of these funds is indicated by the landmark decision in *Mills* v. *D.C. Board of Education:*

> If sufficient funds are not available to finance all of the services and programs that are needed and desirable in the system, then the available funds must be expended equitably in such a manner that no child is entirely excluded from a publicly supported education. . . . The inadequacies of the . . . Public School System whether occasioned by insufficient funding or administrative inefficiency, certainly cannot be permitted to bear more heavily on the "exceptional" or handicapped child than on the normal child.[9]

In practice, in many school districts, insufficient funding for federally mandated programs is being borne more heavily by nonhandicapped children than by handicapped children. When full funding is not possible, the financial shortfall should be shared equally by handicapped and nonhandicapped students. The fiscal and civil rights questions inherent in the issue of educational and physical accommodations for the handicapped will continue to have serious public policy consequences in the 1980s.

Bilingual Education. In 1968 and 1978, Congress authorized funds to support bilingual education for students who did not understand English well enough to learn successfully when taught in that language. In a 1974 decision, *Lau* v. *Nichols,*[10] the Supreme Court established the principle that equality of educational opportunity is not provided by simply offering the same facilities, textbooks, teachers, and curriculum. Schools must now adapt their curricula to accommodate new educational approaches that make learning easier for "limited-English-proficient" students.

The teaching of English as a Second Language (ESL) is one approach to this goal. However, although ESL has been shown to teach English effectively, it addresses only one of two critical student needs during the period of transition to full English skills. Transitional bilingual education is an alternative model that provides for both the acquisition of English language skills and the development of students' cognitive skills during the achievement of English proficiency. Some Panel members support transitional bilingual education.

Other Panel members, including the Chairman, do not support this particular approach. A key element of any bilingual program, these members believe, is the assurance that the children receiving instruction will spend as much time as possible with other children to promote integration and avoid segregation from their peers. If classes providing

82

language programs foster segregation, it is the school authority's duty and responsibility to remedy the isolation.

By 1985, the United States will have the fifth largest population of Spanish-speaking people in the Western hemisphere, as well as a broad new ethnic mixture of immigrants and refugees. This Panel concurs with recent reports that have highlighted the benefits to this nation of an international perspective in an increasingly interdependent world. Schools can help young people develop a more sensitive understanding of cultural differences through a more deliberate use of multicultural and multilingual curricula.

Pre-Elementary Education. One-half of all children between 3 and 5 years old were enrolled in preschool programs in 1978; a majority were in public school programs. Significant enrollment increases were recorded for the children of both working and nonworking mothers. There has been a 65 percent increase since 1965 in the number of preschool children whose mothers work; that trend is expected to continue in the 1980s.[11] It seems clear that the need for pre-elementary education will grow in the coming decade beyond that indicated by simple population growth. A recent, respected analysis of longitudinal data from early-education programs for low-income children supports the continued development of these programs.[12] Federal, state, and local support for pre-elementary education may be the first step toward school improvement.

The problems of public schools are most acute in central city districts. The general condition of education for low-income blacks, Hispanics, and native Americans, especially in central cities, remains staggeringly deficient. Handicaps inherent to the economic circumstances of poor and minority families are fundamental causes of problems that can limit a child's ability to take advantage of traditional school programs. City schools show absentee and dropout rates that far exceed the national medians, while their students' achievement test results are much lower than average. Evidence indicates that compensatory education programs will help these disadvantaged students;[13] but more can and should be done.

A number of suggestions toward this end have been offered. Some members of the Panel believe that school districts might experiment with a project that would test the merits of extending high school from 4 to 6 years for those students who want to work more than part-time. By combining education and work in a flexible arrangement, this project would be of real assistance in enabling students to complete high school. It would also help to generate public school collaboration with the employment and training sectors and with community colleges.

City Schools

Other Panel members, including the Chairman, point out that jobs are scarce for minority youths who lack a high school diploma. Instead of helping these young people, the experiment might encourage them to leave school and thereby reduce their chances of permanent employment. The push-out and drop-out rates for elementary and secondary school students is escalating in city schools. An extension of time for them to complete high school may exacerbate this problem.

Another useful innovation might be the creation of intermediate level, regionally organized educational service units with combined federal and state support. These units could provide those services that cannot be offered efficiently by any one district, reduce individual districts' administrative costs, and might also serve as a legitimate and effective liaison with organizations outside the school system.

Safety in the Schools

Student misbehavior, lack of interest, disrespect for teachers and rules, and other difficulties of classroom management have long been problems in American education. In the past decade, however, public concern with crime, violence, and drugs in the schools has heightened. In the mid-1970s, the Senate Subcommittee to Investigate Juvenile Delinquency noted mounting evidence of school violence and vandalism.[14] Newspapers and the other media have presented stories of violent encounters in schools and massive property destruction. Parents, teachers, and school administrators have voiced serious concern about the problem. In 1978, the cost of repairing the damage from vandalism nationwide was $600 million—three times the cost in 1971.[15] As a consequence, some school districts have allocated large sums of money for school security— money that is sorely needed for other educational purposes. The maintenance of a safe and secure learning environment, with a reduction in expenditures for security measures, is a serious concern for schools and communities in the 1980s.

Summary

The role of the public schools in meeting the needs of students who require special services has changed considerably over the past 40 years. The average number of years of schooling for members of minority groups almost doubled between 1940 and 1970; school enrollment figures for handicapped children have risen from 164,000 in 1940 to 3,158,000 in 1978, an increase of nearly 2,000 percent; and the number of pupils who do not speak English has risen dramatically, and is expected to continue to rise.[16] The cost of supplementary services has increased rapidly as the courts broadened the applicability of civil rights legislation

84

and as state and local education agencies sought to comply with judicial directives.

The federal government has supported the improvement of educational services for economically and educationally disadvantaged students. The Panel believes that now—when the birth rate of the poor will continue to be twice that of the nonpoor, when the number of teenage pregnancies is increasing rapidly, when evidence indicates that compensatory education is effective, and when the minority youth unemployment rate is about three times that of white youth—is the time for federal education policy to reaffirm its central mission of promoting access and opportunity for the disadvantaged.

Collaboration. One of the telling criticisms of the public school system is that it attempts a degree of self-containment that is neither appropriate nor useful in an increasingly interdependent world. More collaboration is needed both within and without the institutional educational network if the needs of today's students are to be served.

Improving the System

With respect to vocational education, for example, some Panel members suggest that vocational education, most of which now takes the form of school-based job-specific skill training, be transferred to the community and technical college level. Other Panel members, including the Chairman, doubt the efficacy of this idea; they fear that this may be one way in which blacks and other minority groups are consigned to vocational education and are blocked from further advancement. Specific occupational skills are increasingly quickly outdated—people will change jobs frequently in the future, and therefore need training in transferable skills, abilities, and attitudes. Public schools cannot afford the kinds of equipment necessary to prepare young people adequately for many of the fast-growing, better-paying occupations; few teenagers really want to make a career choice at the age of 15 or 16; and private industry is more likely to accept extensive involvement with community colleges than with high schools. This proposal calls for an effective collaboration between secondary schools and community colleges and permits selective high school student participation in community college vocational education.

Present vocational education funds would be better used for high school programs with diverse learning options and community-based, work-related experiences. The principal target of these programs would be those disadvantaged and other youth who reject the traditional school structure, are not now enrolled in vocational programs, and have considerable difficulty in finding jobs.

85

An additional source of money for such programs would be the collaborative school/CETA programs authorized by the federal Youth Employment Demonstration Projects Act of 1977 and the Department of Education's proposed $1 billion secondary school Youth Employability Initiative. Schools could thus provide the two elements considered essential to improving the employment chances of high-risk, disadvantaged youths: competence in basic education skills and work/community-related learning experiences. Specific skill training would be offered by institutions better able to provide it.

The Panel believes that the "private pursuit of public interests"[17] is an important element of school improvement in the 1980s. Organizations and individuals should be encouraged to offer their help to the public schools. For example, in "adopt-a-school" programs, businesses donate books, establish vocational programs, and allow employees time to volunteer in the schools. Citizens might be given incentives to provide volunteer services in specified schools, and chambers of commerce might sponsor school improvement advertising campaigns. When it has been tried, such involvement of the private sector in the improvement of public schools has provided tangible and intangible benefits worth many times the direct costs involved. That involvement must be expanded.

A spirit of innovation, a willingness to experiment, will be needed. Public schools can benefit substantially from networks that link the public schools to parents, businesses, labor unions, industry, community organizations, cultural agencies, private schools, and postsecondary schools. These networks could fill the need for a continuous interchange between the public and the schools, laying the foundation for the development of a school site council—a group of school and community representatives concerned with a particular school. The council would have decisionmaking authority in areas such as program planning, structural changes, and the use of federal funds.

Testing

The quality of teaching is difficult to measure. Since 1976, however, 38 states have made an attempt to establish minimum standards of learning by requiring that students pass standardized tests of minimum competency in order to be promoted or graduated. Proponents of this form of testing think that the inability of the school to accomplish its many objectives, and declining achievement tests scores, are adequate reasons for establishing minimum standards. Opponents of minimum competency tests question the criteria used to establish a minimum level of competency; they point to cultural bias as just one of many limitations to test scores in the evaluation of achievement and aptitude. They also fear that minimum competencies might become accepted maximum competencies, thereby resulting in a further lowering of educational standards.

Norm-referenced standardized achievement tests are also controversial. Widely used, misused, and often misinterpreted, norm-referenced tests do not help teachers diagnose learning problems and are used primarily as sorting and screening devices. Criterion-referenced achievement tests, on the other hand, allow the analysis of whether children or groups of children have learned particular knowledge and skills that are taught by the school. They can be immensely helpful to the classroom teacher and the administrator as a guide to correct and accelerate student learning.

The Panel recommends that standardized achievement testing be reevaluated by the nation's most gifted social scientists. Tests should be seen as a tool for diagnosing students' abilities and disabilities, as a basis for supplying additional resources and individualized attention as early and as often as needed, and as one of a number of factors in grade promotion and graduation decisions. Early consideration should be given to the design of new tests, to the calibration of existing tests, and to the training of the teachers who will use them.

Basic Skills

Although the first years of schooling usually provide a solid foundation in basic skills, it has been found that remedial instruction is often needed in the junior and senior high school years. In partial response, the "back-to-basics" movement, a concerted effort to force the public schools to focus their attention and resources on teaching the fundamental skills of reading, writing, and ciphering, emerged in the early 1970s. It is directly related to the institution of minimum competency testing and motivated by the same concerns. There have been unusually large numbers of students during the past decade with low test scores; in certain areas of deprivation, such as central city districts, the conditions are substantially worse. Accordingly, the Panel believes that schools should:

☐ Continue to emphasize basic skills achievement at the elementary school level;
☐ Retrain teachers in the diagnosis and remediation of basic skills deficiencies at the elementary and secondary school level;
☐ Provide basic skills centers and individualized skill packets;
☐ Use parents as volunteers to augment emphasis on basic skills;

☐ Provide credit for relevant learning experiences outside classrooms in order to help students understand how coursework and basic skills are related to adult responsibilities.

A number of reports indicate that there are limits to the ability of the public schools, when other social forces (e.g., television) are considered, to affect the educational fortunes of its students.[18] However, if many of this nation's young people continue to be inadequately prepared in the basic skills, both social justice and productivity will be diminished.

This Panel must also caution against overemphasizing basic skills. Abuse occurs when "back-to-basics" is used as an excuse to block other curriculum and programmatic development, to eliminate "frills" in order to reduce school budgets, or as a means of constraining school personnel. For example, both "back-to-basics" and tax-cutting rhetoric often result in calls for cutbacks in what are seen by some as frills and by others as important elements of the school program. If schools without "frills" (such as art, music, foreign languages, after-school activities, books, and personal instruction) become the standard pattern, especially in financially burdened cities, then public schools will again become "poor schools," as they were called before the advent of universal access to public education. There is a growing belief that "back-to-basics" is a code phrase for teaching the minimum, for lower achievement expectations, and for avoiding the moral and other developmental needs of children. Concern for basic skills achievement should not compromise the need for diversity and enrichment in school curricula.

Teaching and Excellence

Testimony from the Panel's public hearings, as well as recent opinion polls, suggests that teacher morale is at its lowest point. A major task for the 1980s is to communicate a message of support to many caring, effective teachers while simultaneously sending firm messages of dissatisfaction to those teachers who are indifferent or ineffective. At present, neither group is receiving a clear message or adequate training.

Teacher training programs (many of which are supported, in part or in whole, by federal funds) should be critically reviewed and reorganized if necessary; and a greater emphasis should be placed on in-service training. Teachers' salaries must be competitive to attract talented, well-trained entrants to the profession—and to keep good teachers in the schools. At the same time, new procedures for monitoring performance should be established in order to relieve the school system of those teachers who are indifferent, ineffective, and unwilling (or unable) to improve. Taxpayers, through local school boards, have a right to hold school personnel accountable for the academic achievement of the students.

A primary concern should be the encouragement of an atmosphere of learning, growth, and mutual respect in which the basic obligations and rights of both students and teachers are fully understood. In this context, equal employment opportunity for minorities and women must remain a priority for the educational system. This goal should continue to be a consideration in all established practices for the hiring and tenure of teachers.

Federal and state education agencies may wish to explore the possibility of establishing a program to award grants to school districts that demonstrate overall school improvement, linkages with public and private organizations, student achievement, teaching excellence, the practical application of curriculum and instructional research, and the dissemination of programs. Such a proposal could correct the unfortunate tendency of current federal education legislation to encourage school districts to emphasize their deficiencies in order to receive assistance. This proposed shift in emphasis will be an incentive to school personnel to demonstrate quality, to regain self-esteem, and to restore public confidence after almost 20 years of crises.

It is commonly held by educators and the public that the school curriculum has become less rigorous, that standards and expectations for both the staff and the students are lower than they used to be. Many teachers have lost their inventiveness and many students have lost confidence in their teachers and schools. School administrators must expect more from the teachers and teachers must expect more from their students. Above all, many educators say, teachers must begin to take more personal responsibility for students' successes and failures. To this end, the Panel recommends the following:

- ☐ First, fundamental learning skills should be taught by using methods that take into account how children differ in their modes and rates of learning, thereby enhancing the opportunities of both the most advanced and the least able students;
- ☐ Second, more resources—whether for "basics" or accelerated learning—should be devoted to adolescents; and
- ☐ Third, the talents of promising and high-achieving students must be given full scope.

It will be tragic if the United States is unable or unwilling to support all three goals.

The Changing Needs of American Youth. One of the most obvious, and fundamental, effects of the events of the past 20 or 30 years is an alteration in the structure of the American family. More than 18 percent of the nation's schoolchildren now live with one parent; 12 million children's parents have been divorced. A recent national study has concluded that children who live with only one parent, for whatever reason, encounter significantly more academic and disciplinary problems than do children who live with both parents.[19]

The circumstances of older children's lives have changed in other ways as well. Today's young people have become much better acquainted with the world outside their communities because of better transportation systems and the omnipresent television. More youths work part-time, at earlier ages, than ever before; their wages help to generate a youth consumer capacity estimated at $4 billion in 1980.[20] Changes in the family, in sexual habits, and in publicly accepted standards for mass media are just a few of the influences that have altered perceptions and behavior and that permit young people partial entry into the adult world.

Possibly the most significant condition affecting young people is a lack of significant and legitimate social, economic, and political roles in their families, institutions, and communities. Without valued tasks to perform, without responsibility or authority, young people become immersed in the affairs of peer groups and create a kind of subculture. This subculture has few ties to reality and its adherents are not especially satisfied.

The Schools' Response

The structure and operation of public schools have changed very little in response to the altered needs of their students. Citizenship skills such as participation and negotiation are rarely learned or practiced within the school by any but a few; nor are they learned or practiced in real world settings. Students can see contradictions between the principles of their civics textbooks and the actual response of the school and the community to their needs for responsibility. Too often students respond with disinterest, apathy, and cynicism. To the extent that students are unable to experience well-planned and supervised community-based learning programs, their needs will be poorly served.

Many educators point to studies that indicate that schools in which students have genuine responsibilities have significant and positive effects on adolescent learning.[21] School philosophy and structure, however, continue to emphasize the primacy of learning in self-contained settings such as the classroom. Many parents and teachers

90

believe that a balance of "real world" experiences and classroom theory is essential to prepare teenagers for adult work, citizenship, and family responsibilities. They testify that students' determination to study increases as they develop a more sophisticated understanding of the correlation between education, employment, community status, and life style choices.[22]

A Suggested Response

There is an important federal and state role in promoting the development of local schools' response to the citizenship, service, and employability needs of youth. Existing federal education legislation provides funds for innovative practices, a function that the states could be performing as well.

Some Panel members propose that part of this money be spent on demonstration projects that would contain a new school sequence for the years now spent in kindergarten through senior high school[23] as well as specific reforms for secondary schools. These suggestions emphasize the acquisition of basic skills during the early grades and some major changes in the nature of a high school education. Indeed, changing the nature of the adolescent schooling experience may be the solution to sustaining the benefits of effective elementary school teaching.

The new sequence comprises a basic, a middle, and a transition school. In the basic school, each pupil would learn to read, write, and speak with clarity and to compute accurately within the limits of his ability. Children would also learn that people communicate with music, theatre, dance, and the visual arts as well as with words. The middle school would offer a rigorous completion of basic school training and a common knowledge of history, global studies, future studies, and human relations. By teaching a core of knowledge and by offering students (who are at a time of great change in their lives) ample opportunity for community-based, active learning, the middle school might reform the stultification in current junior high schools. The transition school would allow students to specialize or to experiment in "school within a school" programs such as advanced placement courses or programs in such fields as health professions, arts, business, or social service. Each program would be linked with public and private community resources. All students would have the opportunity to test their skills, pursue special interests, and explore career options.

Specific secondary school reforms include a counseling program that integrates personal and career guidance with educational planning. Counseling services must be expanded to reach more than just those students with behavior or course scheduling problems.

91

Incentives, such as independent study and inter-disciplinary programs, should be given to all students but especially to the average student who does not earn special attention for being very good or bad. Students should be evaluated and promoted by a procedure that is based on mastery of subject matter, not on time in class or years in school. Students would progress at their own rates in learning what the school has set out to teach.

Other Panel members, including the Chairman, do not wish to discourage educational innovation. They feel, however, that some of the proposed reforms favored by their fellow Panel members will only serve to mask more basic problems with the educational system. In particular, they find that the proposal to restructure the schools may be only a bureaucratic innovation, one that ultimately proves of little value to students. Creation of a basic school, for example, will not in and of itself mean that students will learn to read, write, or speak with clarity. To achieve that monumental task, these Panel members believe, something more fundamental is required.

One opportunity to broaden the character of secondary schooling is offered by a proposal to institute a voluntary youth service project. Established by each state and supported with matching federal funds, this voluntary youth service program would be administered through public secondary schools and be open to students 14 to 18 years of age. During the school term, students would commit themselves to a period of service for which they could receive credit toward graduation. Skills such as cross-age and peer tutoring and assignments in social service agencies would be emphasized. Such a service program (variations of which are successfully in place in California, Maryland, and Detroit) would complement the usual academic training and could strengthen its meaning for students. It might also inspire the enthusiasm that is needed to recapture the imagination of this nation's youth. For all these reasons, some Panel members favor experimentation with a voluntary youth service project.

Other Panel members, including the Chairman, fear that such a project might produce undesirable results. They note that the precedents for such a service come from experiences that the United States does not seek to emulate. The concept of youth service can be easily abused and become a means by which politicians gain favor with youth. These Panel members believe that the school system should concentrate on improving the academic achievement of its students, not on youth service programs.

A Further Response: The Concept of Service

Demographic Trends. One reason for some of the public schools' difficulties is the absence of planning for future demographic and social changes. Many school systems learned during the 1970s that it costs much more to react to changes than to anticipate them. In the 1980s, certain demographic and social trends will bear heavily on the education system. Continuing a decade of decline, the number of elementary school-age children is expected to drop another 4 percent in the early 1980s and then begin to increase. By 1990, there should be approximately as many children between the ages of 5 and 13 as there were in 1960. Racial minority representation in this cohort will be 17.7 percent in 1990, compared to an expected racial minority representation of 14.8 percent in the total population in 1990. In general, the "Sunbelt" areas of the South and West will see smaller reductions and greater increases in elementary school enrollments than will other regions.

The number of young people of high school age is expected to decline about 19 percent during the 1980s. Racial minority representation in the 14-year-old to 17-year-old cohort will probably increase to 19.4 percent in 1990. The representation of Hispanics in both the younger and older age groups is expected to grow more rapidly than either the black or majority populations. For both age groups, the pattern of enrollment decline and recovery will vary greatly from locality to locality, principally because of differential migration.[24]

*Local School
Finances*

The traditional reliance on the local real property tax as the main source of financing of public schools is breaking down as a result of court decisions that follow the lead of *Serrano* v. *Priest*.[25] The *Serrano* decision declared that heavy reliance on local property taxes was unconstitutional because it denied equal protection under the law to children living in low-income districts. Other factors that operate to reduce reliance on property taxes include refusals by local taxpayers to vote for school tax measures; the problems of central cities, which have forced the schools to fight a difficult, frequently losing battle for local funds in competition with other public sector needs; a sharply reduced proportion of families with school-age children and a larger proportion of retired citizens—that is, a smaller constituency; the nationwide growth of collective bargaining among education employees, which has resulted in the flow of a larger proportion of any increases in school district revenues into mandated compensation for school personnel; and the impact of inflation and rising fuel costs on educational budgets.

The cost of public schooling has continued to rise despite declining enrollments. School costs have risen 187 percent compared to an 80 percent increase in consumer costs over the past 10 years. Teachers' salaries represent approximately 65 percent of total school expenditures.[26] Rising school costs have reflected general salary increases; a higher proportion of tenured teachers; the cost of specially trained teachers and other added services required for state and federally mandated programs; and the growing costs of pensions, unemployment insurance, and other fringe benefits. In addition, heating oil, paper, electricity, and other items of substantial consequence to school budgets were among the commodities exhibiting the most rapid price increases.

The decline in school enrollments, which might have been expected to help free funds for increased per-pupil expenditures, has not had that result in many communities. State support, and some federal allocations, are based on average daily attendance figures and tend to decline, at least in constant dollars, when enrollment falls. Few school districts have used enrollment decline to reduce class size despite abundant evidence supporting the positive effect of small classes on learning. In addition, while managing contraction, school administrators must assess each decision in terms of its consequences for increased enrollment in the future. Sometimes these considerations are mutually conflicting.

The management of decline must be handled differently in different geographic areas. In urban areas, for example, the costs of educating students are higher than they are in the suburbs. There is a greater need, and consequently higher costs, for special education, remedial instruction, medical and social services, and building maintenance. The financial base of urban schools is diminishing as their objective needs grow larger. Cities are losing their ability to generate revenues for the schools and often receive an unsympathetic response from state legislatures to requests for state aid. To an extent unknown in nonurban areas, city schools increasingly must compete with other vital public services for each local tax dollar raised. In the 1980s, urban school finance issues should be considered in the context of intergovernmental finances, and urban education policy decisions should be made within the context of general urban policy decisions.

The 1980s are likely to be a period when school districts will, out of necessity, turn to new and improved management practices, diversified services, and flexible personnel policies. State education departments could assist urban schools by reformulating state aid policies to mitigate the effects of sudden enrollment losses, and by providing technical assistance in management and planning. Smaller, less sophisticated districts could also benefit from these state initiatives.

94

The critical need is the resolution of the conflicts among rising educational costs, higher expectations, and mounting voter resistance to higher taxes. While the Panel recognizes that schools may often have to do more with less, it also believes that it is inevitable and necessary that public education funding increase in the 1980s. The Panel realizes that school budget decisions will be closely scrutinized, but wishes to emphasize that the potential for school improvement will diminish and the drift to private schools could strengthen if local school districts do not increase educational funding. Where needed budget increases continue to be rejected, the Panel believes that state governments have a responsibility to intervene to ensure an adequate public investment in the education of our nation's youth.

From 1945 to 1970, state funds constituted approximately 40 percent of all revenues allotted to public elementary and secondary schools. The major purpose of these funds was to ensure a minimum level of school expenditures in each school district. That purpose was contravened to the extent that each state's share was not the same (for example, Washington contributed 71 percent of local school costs; New Hampshire contributed only 9.5 percent). School finance reformers, supported by *Serrano, Rodriguez,* and other judicial decisions, have attempted to make school spending independent of property values in order to reduce the gap in per-pupil expenditures between wealthy and poor school districts.[27] For example, in 1975 Massachusetts had an expenditure disparity index of 2.2, indicating that a school district near the top in terms of per-pupil expenditures spent more than twice as much as a district near the bottom. School finance studies have indicated that as the state share of school spending (which rose to 47 percent in 1979) has increased relative to local support, the disparities in expenditures per pupil have been reduced.

School Finance Reform

Property tax revenues now constitute about 15 percent of total state and local revenues, down from 26 percent in 1965. Experts widely agree that the methods used in assessment are often irrational and inefficient, that the residential property tax falls hardest on those with low incomes, and that heavy reliance on property tax revenues creates serious disparities between the needs of a community and its ability to finance necessary services. As a result, there is a clear trend toward increased state use of personal and corporate income taxes as well as federal general revenue sharing funds—a trend that is widely thought to decrease relative tax burdens on the poor. State surpluses, which often paid for the costs of increased state shares, are expected to dwindle in the 1980s while tax limitation movements militate against future school finance reforms.[28]

The voucher system and tuition tax credits are two of a number of proposals under discussion to develop alternative school financing methods. Advocates believe that these proposals would encourage greater consumer accountability and choice, and promote a competitive incentive to improve school quality. Those opposed to the use of public funds in support of private education fear that such efforts would impair and contravene the nation's historic commitment to universally available, free education and equality of opportunity. The education agenda for the 1980s should include an examination of the consequences of the policy choices for and against vouchers, tax credits, and other means of channeling public funds to the private sector of education. The options require extended study by a competent and objective body of public policy experts outside the frame of partisan politics.

Adequate financing alone is not the answer to improved education, but helping poorer school districts provide better educational services is an essential element in the improvement of education and the advancement of social justice. Many states have already enacted school finance equalization legislation. The Panel recommends that states that have not acted seek reform of their school finance systems in order to make the quality of a student's education less dependent on local taxable wealth. Moreover, in providing financial assistance to local school districts, this legislation should recognize the greater costs that some localities incur because of larger concentrations of disadvantaged families and the higher costs of virtually all services in such areas. Finally, equitable financing of elementary and secondary education, particularly in urban areas, should be regarded by federal and state governments as an integral part of the larger problem of intergovernmental finance.

Changes in Higher Education

There are serious difficulties facing elementary and secondary education; in higher education, the problems do not seem to be so severe. The past decade has witnessed the release of a number of well-known national reports about the future of higher education. Outlined below are some of the more prominent issues and possibilities in higher education in the 1980s.

Demographic Trends

Little uncertainty is involved in projecting the size of the college-age population, which is expected to drop 6 percent (to 27.9 million people) by 1985 and 15 percent (to 25.1 million people) by 1990. Social, economic, and demographic factors that influence actual enrollment in higher education, however, may vary widely.

In 1978, 35 percent of all students enrolled in higher education were more than 24 years old, and 70 percent of them were part-time students. This percentage will grow over the next 10 years when the population over the age of 24 will increase by more than 22 million. College campuses in 1990 will include a vastly greater proportion of women and minority students. Students are expected to continue to move away from studies in the social sciences and the humanities into career-oriented departments such as business or engineering. The changing student profile also suggests the likelihood of renewed student demands for greater participation in college governance—now from a more focused, consumer's perspective.

The most significant factor contributing to changes in the faculty profile during the coming decade will be changes in the age distribution of professors. It is projected that the average age of faculty members will be 55 in 1990, and the proportion under the age of 35 will decline from 28 percent in 1970 to 4 percent in 1990.[29]

Financial and Structural Problems

It appears that higher education supported its operations throughout the 1970s by consuming its capital base: its physical, financial, and, particularly, its human capital. In the 1980s, colleges and universities will be faced with declining enrollments, escalating costs, faculty unions, and increased competition from private industry. Declining enrollments and tight budgets will not affect all areas of the country equally, but many institutions will be forced to terminate or trim certain programs of study. And there will be sharp competition in recruiting students, because of the federal and state financial support that accompanies most new students. A critical issue for higher education institutions in the 1980s is how to ensure that they will retain the financial and physical capabilities to perform teaching, research, and other services with quality and integrity.

Programmatic adaptations and marketing schemes are becoming common ways to attract more students. Many educators are hoping that growing numbers of older students will compensate for the decline in the traditional student population; however, most older, adult students are part-time, and they are most often enrolled in fields of study in which faculty are least numerous and most overworked. In most institutions, the expected rise in part-time enrollments will not be enough to offset full-time enrollment decreases.

Even in institutions that do not experience the effects of enrollment decline, a rise in the percentage of tenured professors, faculty salaries, and other costs will create austere budgetary conditions. For example, at one Midwestern university, 85 percent of the faculty members are tenured and earn comparatively high salaries. The real salaries of faculty members have declined by 18.4 percent since 1970.[30] It is this erosion of salaries that presages increased faculty demands and casts doubt upon the ability of academic institutions to compete with the private sector for well-trained, creative, and highly qualified individuals.

Of particular concern are private liberal arts colleges that are already in serious financial crises. These schools have trimmed their operating budgets in an attempt to achieve maximum efficiency and to absorb inflationary cost increases without sacrificing educational excellence. Many of these institutions are threatened by the college-age population decline and by competition from well-endowed private colleges. Private college leaders feel that the current maximum federal student grant levels (Pell grants) actually serve as an inducement for students to attend low-cost public institutions,* and are discouraged by the response to their appeals for state assistance (state legislatures normally have a greater interest in the success of public institutions of higher education). Private colleges could be strengthened if existing State Coordinating Commissions on Higher Education convened forums in which both public and private institutions might attempt to reconcile competing interests—not simply in terms of institutional survival, but rather with a view toward advancing their shared purpose.

Equal Educational Opportunity

In discussions of discrimination at the postsecondary level, much has been made of the fact that the proportion of minority high school graduates going to college is now approximately the same as that of whites. However, this hopeful sign must be qualified by three reservations. First, there is a much higher dropout rate from high school for blacks than for whites; therefore, in the group graduating from high school, blacks are under-represented. Second, the national unemployment rate for white high school dropouts is lower than the unemployment rate for black college graduates. Third, the colleges and universities most minority students attend are different from those attended by most whites; they are predominantly low-cost, low-status institutions, and frequently community colleges. More than one-half of Hispanic and native American students attended public 2-year colleges in 1978, compared to 39 percent of black students and only one-third of white students.[31] A growing concern expressed by minority group leaders is that a new form of segregation by type of

---

* Student aid programs are generally praised for their contribution to equal access to higher education. The Panel agrees with this purpose.

institution is occurring. This will be the subject of civil rights litigation in the 1980s.

Desegregation in higher education will also remain a heated issue in the 1980s as a result of the *Adams* decision and the *Bakke* ruling.[32] In *Adams,* 10 states were alleged to have dual (racially identifiable) systems of postsecondary education. These states were charged with noncompliance with Title VI of the Civil Rights Act of 1964. Only half of the 10 states have complied with the suggested guidelines. In concurrence with the major concerns addressed in this case, the Panel supports the strengthening of historically black colleges and the elimination of any program duplication between historically white and black institutions in states maintaining "dual systems;" the achievement of an equitable enrollment of minority students in desegregated institutions; and an increase in the representation of black faculty and administrators in desegregated institutions and on institutional governing boards.

Although historically black colleges make up only 5 percent of the total number of U.S. colleges and universities, they confer 38 percent of all the baccalaureate degrees granted to black students.[33] In order to offer historically black colleges and universities an equal opportunity in the economic life of the higher education community and an improved ability to provide their students with a quality education, the Panel recommends an increase in the participation by these colleges and universities in current federal programs.

It is likely that many affirmative action cases will appear in the 1980s. The Panel supports the use of affirmative action to remedy past discrimination.

Research

One of the principal features of higher education in this country has been continued federal assistance for basic and applied research. The Land Grant College Act of 1862 and the associated amendments that established the "1890 colleges" stimulated research in agricultural and mechanical sciences. Since that time, university-based research has been vital to the progress of this nation. In 1968, federal legislation created the first urban land grant institution, Federal City College in the District of Columbia, in the hope that the land grant spirit and success in solving agricultural and technical problems could be applied to the solution of urban . problems. The Higher Education Amendments of 1980 will facilitate this effort. The bill establishes an Urban University Grants Program in an effort to apply the expertise of urban universities to problems in the surrounding communities. The endeavor will fall short of its goal, however, if it is not carried out with heightened sensitivity to the concerns of the members of those communities.

Current national problems, including the decline in world economic competitiveness, may be resolved in part by renewing the national commitment to the spirit of the Land Grant Act and increasing federal and state funds for research in institutions of higher education. Indeed, the strength and diversity of the American higher education system undergirds the strength and diversity of the American political, economic, and social systems.

In 1978, 34 percent of all college students attended public 2-year postsecondary institutions. The flexibility and durability of these schools are noteworthy. The community college is readily accessible to the community or communities it serves, has a tuition which is much lower than that of 4-year institutions, and has disproportionately large numbers of minority students, the result in part of limited access to 4-year colleges.

Community Colleges

Many community college leaders would like to see a redefinition of purpose in which their schools become known as community learning centers rather than as "mini" 4-year colleges. Community college leaders plan for the future in terms of the job-related and personal needs of adult learners, although traditional academic training is also offered. Some interest groups have expressed the concern that community colleges are becoming the highest educational institution many students attend. They fear that a decreased emphasis on academic courses will not only hinder students' chances of transferring to 4-year institutions, but also will fail to meet these students' educational needs.

Community colleges have the capability to respond to the specific needs of corporations, community organizations, CETA projects, labor unions, and the elderly, as well as the remedial and advanced placement needs of high school students. Two hundred community colleges, for example, have forged relationships with labor unions to establish joint apprenticeship committees that will oversee the training of new employees. If the current response to community colleges continues, these schools may represent one of the most successful and productive innovations in higher education in the 1980s.

Public schools have always depended on colleges to prepare teachers. Colleges are now increasingly dependent upon the quality of elementary and secondary educational institutions. The quality of preparation of entering college students determines the amount of time needed for instructional remediation and, to some extent, affects the morale of college faculty. Yet most colleges are reluctant to accept

Higher Education and the Problems of Public Schools

100

their full part in the relationship, by, for example, improving teacher education programs.

Colleges should urge their gifted students to teach young children and should promote research in teaching and learning and devote some of their community service efforts to public schools. To recover lost credibility with local public schools and to help solve a national problem, colleges and universities must demonstrate their will and their ability to help improve the performance and effectiveness of local schools.

The U.S. education system is severely fragmented by multiple differences. Special interest group advocacy and the frequent use of litigation to resolve disputes have had the unintended consequence of fostering factionalism in public education to such an extent that compromise and consensus are almost obsolete. In an era of fiscal and social conservatism, such conditions are often used in an attempt to justify a decreased investment in public education.

This dissidence was not conducive to learning or excellence in public education in the 1970s, nor was it conducive to the scientific, technological, and economic growth that is stimulated by a thriving education system. Indeed, throughout the 1970s, educators and other social commentators have been focusing on "survival" of public education as the theme around which all other issues revolve. Although there are understandable reasons for this perspective, the mentality it engenders is debilitating, and produces defensive rather than innovative educational policies and practices. It inhibits talent and potential and is the antithesis of the response that is needed to improve the quality of public education.

The Panel believes that the most effective responses in the 1980s may well be those that incorporate four approaches woven throughout this report. For students, staff, parents, and the public, many of whom are alienated, the means recommended here will be critical to restoring confidence in public schools and the achievement of equality, competence, and excellence. In summary form, they are:

□ *Collaboration.* School functions should be supplemented with voluntary efforts by private and public community organizations. There must be a concerted effort, especially in urban areas, from different levels of government and the private sector to demonstrate a concern and a responsibility for the educational development of young people.

□ *Incentives.* Where pleas for civic responsibility are not heeded, a variety of incentives should be used.

The Prospect

101

☐ *Staff and leadership development.* School improvement will be aided by the research and development of new ideas in school organization, teaching, and learning. As the demands on public schools have increased, the teachers' need for periodic retraining has become critical. The similar needs of school leaders—senior administrators and lay leaders—must also be answered.

☐ *Citizenship and student participation.* Students should be offered meaningful roles within their schools and communities. Students are expected to become more responsible citizens; they should be provided with opportunities to observe a new civic morality in which the community initiates and responds to cooperative involvement with the schools.

Financial, structural, and programmatic changes are necessary but not sufficient to remedy the problems and the malaise in public education. Three additional challenges are apparent.

First, a positive image of schools and youth as resources, not as problems, should be revived. Second, public education should respond to social needs by clearly separating that which it can accomplish alone, that which it cannot accomplish, and that which it can accomplish only with collaboration from one or more outside organizations. The 1980s may find the public school system less willing to claim total credit for accomplishments and more willing to acknowledge and use the power of nonschool resources.

Third, the administration of public schools should be the responsibility of people who can lead as well as manage. Managers excel in the ability to handle the routine, but rarely ask whether the routine should be done at all. Although educational administrators are often perceptive about the resolutions of their problems, too few are willing to act on those perceptions, and too few believe that their decisions can shape the course of future actions.

The task of restoring confidence and quality in public schools requires leaders who have the skills to mediate among factions in a way that produces a constructive consensus. At the same time, the future of public education will require leaders who not only can improve school quality, but can also market school quality, in an increasingly competitive and distrustful public arena. Leadership of this caliber will help keep in the public mind the truth that effective education of all children is a public good, and that society ultimately pays for ignorance and social injustice just as it pays for disease and crime. In the 1980s, education's leaders, teachers, parents, and students, in concert with the larger community, must work together to realize the full promise of public education.

1. U.S. Department of Education, National Center for Education Statistics, *Digest of Education Statistics* (Washington, D.C., 1980), pp. 175-179.
2. *Ibid.*
3. *Brown* v. *Board of Education of Topeka,* 347 U.S. 483 (1954).
4. Private communication from David Soule, Pupil Transportation and Safety Specialist, U.S. Department of Transportation (Washington, D.C., September 1980).
5. *Milliken* v. *Bradley,* 418 U.S. 717 (1974).
6. U.S. Office of Education, Office of Planning and Budgeting, *Preliminary Budget Request: Fiscal Year 1981. Volume 1: Summary and Overview* (Washington, D.C., 1979); U.S. Department of Education, National Center for Education Statistics, *The Condition of Education* (Washington, D.C., 1980), pp. 44-55.
7. L. Danielson and A. Paller, "Probable Upper Limits on the Number of Handicapped Children in the United States," mimeographed (Washington, D.C., 1978); U.S. Congress, Senate Committee on Labor and Human Resources, Subcommittee on the Handicapped, transcript, testimony of Gregory J. Ahart (Washington, D.C., September 10, 1980).
8. William Schipper, "Financial and Administrative Considerations," *Journal of School Health* (May 1980):288-290.
9. *Mills* v. *D.C. Board of Education,* 348 F.Supp. 866 (D.D.C. 1972).
10. *Lau* v. *Nichols,* 414 U.S. 563 (1974).
11. U.S. Department of Labor, Bureau of Labor Statistics, "Marital and Family Characteristics of Workers," Special Labor Force Report No. 219 (Washington, D.C., 1978).
12. Consortium for Longitudinal Studies, *Summary: Effects After Preschool* (Washington, D.C., 1979).
13. National Institute of Education, *Reports of the NIE Compensatory Education Study* (Washington, D.C., 1977).
14. Birch Bayh, "Seeking Solutions to School Violence and Vandalism," *Phi Delta Kappan* 59, 5:229-302.
15. "School Vandalism: The Bill Is $600 Million a Year," *Senior Scholastic* 110:19-22.
16. Paul A. Pohland, *The New Mexico Principalship Study* (Albuquerque, N.M., 1979).
17. John Gardner, "The Private Pursuit of Public Purpose," *Chronicle of Higher Education* 17:96
18. College Entrance Examination Board, *On Further Examination: Report of the Advisory Panel on the Scholastic Aptitude Test Score Decline* (New York, 1977); National Institute of Education, *Proceedings of the National Conference on Achievement Testing* (Washington, D.C., 1978).
19. "Study of School Needs of Children from One-Parent Families," *Principal* 60, 1:30-40.
20. U.S. Department of Health, Education, and Welfare, Office of Education, *The Urban High School Reform Initiative* (Washington, D.C., 1979), pp. 37-38.
21. Michael Rutter et al., *Fifteen Thousand Hours: Secondary Schools and Their Effects on Children* (Cambridge, Mass., 1979).
22. *Urban High School Reform,* pp. 56-57.
23. Ernest Boyer, *New York Times,* 7 January 1979, p. 14.
24. *Condition of Education,* p. 48.
25. *Serrano* v. *Priest,* 5 Cal.3d 584, 96 Cal.Rptr. 601, 487 P.2d 1241 (1971).
26. William H. Wilken and John J. Callahan, "Declining Enrollment: The Cloud and Its Silver Lining," in *Declining Enrollments,* eds. S. Abramowitz and S. Rosenfeld (Washington, D.C., 1978), pp. 257-304.
27. *San Antonio Independent School District* v. *Rodriguez,* 411 U.S. 1 (1973).

28. James A. Kelly, "Looking Back, Moving Ahead" (Paper read at the Ford Foundation Conference on the Politics of Equity, San Antonio, Texas, May 1980).
29. Carnegie Council on Policy Studies in Higher Education, *Three Thousand Futures* (San Francisco, Calif., 1980).
30. "Report on the Annual Survey of Faculty Compensation, 1977-78," American Association of University Professors *AAUP Bulletin* (September 1980).
31. *Condition of Education,* p. 97.
32. *Adams* v. *Richardson,* 480 F.2d 1159 (D.D.C. 1973); *Regents of the University of California* v. *Bakke,* 438 U.S. 265 (1978).
33. Jimmy Carter, "Remarks on Signing Executive Order 12232, August 8, 1980," *Weekly Compilation of Presidential Documents.*

Chapter 5

THE
Criminal Justice
SYSTEM AND SOCIAL JUSTICE
IN THE 1980s

The scope of the criminal justice system is far broader than many people realize. By some criteria, indeed, the criminal justice system could be considered a major U.S. industry. In 1977, for example, local, state, and federal governments spent more than $21 billion on criminal justice. That year the system employed more than 1.1 million people, a figure comparable to those of the communication and chemical industries. With 10 million arrests, nearly half a million people incarcerated, more than 1 million people on some form of conditional release, and an estimated 53 million criminal incidents, the criminal justice system made a direct impact in some way on the lives of one citizen in every four in 1977.[1]

This analysis is not comprehensive; deterring crime, although an important subject, receives only indirect mention. Instead the Panel chose to concentrate on the social justice aspects of the criminal justice system, and accordingly has emphasized victims' rights, police brutality and use of deadly force, pre-trial release, non-court dispute resolution, and juvenile justice.

The Impacts of Crime: Causes and Prevention

Crime rates have increased dramatically in almost every year since 1960. For example, violent crime (murder, robbery, rape, aggravated assault) increased from 159 persons per 100,000 in 1960, to 363 per 100,000 in 1970, to 466 per 100,000 in 1977. In 1977, someone was the victim of a crime every 3.0 seconds, 24 hours a day, every day. Other forms of crime, such as white-collar crime, are more difficult to detect and assess, and they cost society a great deal; estimates range from $5 billion to $44 billion.[2]

Violent crime threatens city dwellers, the elderly, and members of minority groups more than it does others. People who live in cities with a population of over 250,000 have 4 times the chance of being raped, 14 times the chance of being robbed, and 6 times the chance of being murdered as do residents of cities with less than 10,000 population.[3] The elderly are less likely to be victims of violent crime, but

107

a violent crime or a burglary has far greater impact on an older person than on a younger adult.

The effectiveness of the criminal justice system is an important concern of the black community. Although blacks are only 11.6 percent of the population, they constitute 25.7 percent of all arrests. Crime also victimizes blacks to a greater extent than it does whites. During 1977, blacks were more than twice as likely to be the victims of robbery as were whites—the difference may, in fact, be understated because blacks are less likely than whites to report a crime to the police.[4]

These data on the impacts of crime underline the need to reduce the crime rate in this country. Unfortunately, experts have only a poor understanding of the causes of crime, and they hold out little hope that the level of criminal activity can be reduced during the 1980s. The probability of a person's committing a crime depends partly on such factors as poverty, unemployment, poor educational achievement, drug and alcohol consumption, and unstable family structure. It stands to reason, therefore, that a poor, unemployed high school dropout is more likely to commit a crime than someone who has a job and a college education. In this manner the links between the criminal justice system and the rest of the social agenda become obvious.

Perhaps the strongest factor in explaining variations in the crime rate, however, is age. Individuals 16 to 29 years of age account for 63.5 percent of all arrests for violent crime, though this group constitutes only 35 percent of the population.[5] This group will increase in numbers through the year 1992, and therefore the rate of all types of violent crime can also be expected to increase in the 1980s. This demographic reality means that the government may be unable to reduce crime rates significantly by attacking "root" causes of crime, at least during the 1980s.

Another approach to crime prevention is through changes in law enforcement programs. But aside from some isolated programs—arson prevention task forces, for example—most new law enforcement programs have not produced dramatic results. Increased police patrols and more sophisticated technology cannot be depended upon to reduce crime.

Crime, like most social problems, must be addressed using a variety of approaches, none of which alone promises any sudden solution. Because crime rates will probably rise in the 1980s, it is imperative that the existing system be fairer and more humane.

Many people are involved with the criminal justice system before any one accused of a crime actually comes to trial (less than 20 percent of reported crimes are ever closed by an arrest, and fewer than 1 out of 10 arrests result in a criminal trial).[6] Despite this fact, the pre-trial aspects of the criminal justice system receive less public attention than do dramatic trials or prison riots. The Panel thinks it important, therefore, to examine what happens before trial: the effects on victims, and their rights; the role of law enforcement personnel; the treatment of the accused's right to bail; and the plight of people in jail.

Victims' Rights

The nation needs a continuing sensitivity to the concerns of victims of crime. Compensation programs, for example, deserve more publicity and greater financial support. At present, some state laws restrict the maximum award (usually in the $10,000 range). Others specify that the payments go to the victim's doctors, hospital, or funeral home, but never to the victim. No state provides compensation for property loss. These laws should be liberalized so that society at large realizes the high cost of crime and will be more likely to increase public expenditures designed to reduce the burden of that cost.

The federal government should also encourage the spread of victims' rights programs. Federal effort at program coordination, both locally and nationally, might well lead to significant improvements at relatively low cost. Federally sponsored research to study the effectiveness of such programs would also be useful.

Law Enforcement

Law enforcement agencies constitute the largest component of the criminal justice system. Agency personnel increased by about 20 percent during the past decade, and by 1977 there were nearly three-quarters of a million people in almost 20,000 such agencies throughout the country.[7] The demands of police work have grown in recent years. Described as the only government agency that "makes house calls 24 hours a day," the police are expected to deal with a wide variety of situations, ranging from traffic control to investigating crimes in progress to handling potential suicides.

During the 1980s, the need to evaluate the effectiveness of law enforcement agencies will increase. Unfortunately, law enforcement activity is difficult to measure, and traditional indices such as the number of arrests or the clearance rate (the ratio of arrests to offenses) are inadequate; neither measure deals with the many other functions of law enforcement agencies, such as deterring crime. Other techniques for law enforcement evaluation must be studied. Citizen or household victimization surveys, modeled after the Department of Health and Human Services' Health Interview Survey, might form a basis for such study. The federal role in this research will have to be significant if the effort is to be successful.

For the minority communities of this nation, the quality of police forces is of more than academic interest. It is the members of these communities who live closest to the forces of social unrest that produce both crime and brutality in dealing with crime. These same communities often have the least power to change police practices.

Public attention to the issue of police brutality during the 1970s has led to a number of important reforms: better training for police, the hiring of better qualified applicants, and the use of independent civilian review boards to handle complaints about police misconduct. Most observers agree that in the places where these steps have been taken there has been a decline in the incidence of police brutality reports.

Racial integration of police forces may also contribute to a decline in such subtle forms of police harassment as verbal abuse and frequent identification checks. When black and white officers work together, many racial stereotypes disappear, from both the public and the police officers' minds.

Nonetheless, highly visible, shocking examples of old-style police racism and brutality still remain, illustrated vividly by the events in Miami's black ghetto during the summer of 1980. This kind of police conduct cannot be condoned; efforts must be made to prevent it and it must be prosecuted vigorously whenever it occurs.

The police are authorized to use deadly force in certain circumstances for the maintenance of public order. Many people think they use such force far too often. From 1967 to 1976 civilian deaths caused by police were rather constant, from 300 to 400 a year. This rate is considerably higher than that of the previous 10 years. Analysis of these data reveals an alarming fact: although black males constitute less than 10 percent of the population and approximately one-fourth of the arrests, they account for nearly half of the deaths caused by police shootings. Looked at another way, a black man had about 10 times greater chance of being killed by the police than did a white man.[8] More importantly, incidents of perceived police brutality have often triggered more widespread urban violence.

The Panel supports three reforms to reduce the incidence of unnecessary police killings. First, every police department should establish guidelines that clearly describe the circumstances in which deadly force may be used. The guidelines should state that no officer should discharge his gun except to defend his life or the life of another person and then only after exhausting all other reasonable means. Second, local police departments, with the federal government's assistance, should train officers to follow the department firearms policy. Finally, and most importantly, the policy must be enforced. An independent board that includes civilians should investigate occasions on which a police gun was fired. The board should then impose stiff penalties whenever the firing of the weapon violates the departmental guidelines.

Studies indicate that the number of fatal shootings by police declines when these reforms are adopted.[9] These reforms do not leave police defenseless when their lives are threatened, and they will help to restore public trust in the police.

Pre-trial release of the accused is one of the most important and controversial issues facing the criminal justice system. In most cases the judge has an option to impose bail, which is a cash deposit or a bond insuring the accused's presence in court. Those who cannot afford to post bail are placed in jail to await trial.

Several important and pervasive problems result from the present bail system. First, the bail bond system, a multimillion-dollar-a-year sinecure, tends to corrupt the administration of justice. Unscrupulous bondsmen have sometimes paid judges, police officials, and lawyers to refer cases. Moreover, bondsmen can simply refuse to provide bail, for any reason they choose. In addition, bail-bondsmen have occasionally used ineffective or excessively violent methods to recapture fugitive defendants. The Panel recommends that the role of bondsmen in the criminal justice system be reduced significantly or eliminated.

Second, by its very nature the system discriminates against poor defendants. Many people who are charged with committing a crime do not have the money necessary to pay the bondsman's premium (usually a non-refundable 10 percent of the amount of bail), much less the larger amount of money the court sets as bail. Thus, poor defendants are the ones who most frequently fail to post bail.

This problem has a ripple effect. Poor defendants spend weeks, months, or years in jail awaiting trial because they cannot afford money for bail. During this period they may well lose their jobs; and, at the same time, they cannot prepare their defenses effectively. People without the money to pay bail more frequently plead guilty and more often are found guilty after trial. They are also sentenced to prison and denied probation more frequently than defendants who were free before trial. This is discriminatory, prejudicial, and unacceptable.

Third, judges can easily manipulate the bail system to serve their own ends. If a judge feels that a particular defendant needs "a taste of jail," or if he finds the defendant or the crime charged to be particularly repugnant, he may set bail so high that the defendant is forced into jail.

111

This happened during the civil rights movement in the 1960s, when many Southern judges manipulated the bail system in order to frustrate civil rights demonstrations and to bankrupt the sponsoring organizations.

Finally, many people criticize the bail system because it allows many dangerous defendants out on the street where they have the opportunity to commit other crimes. Under current laws governing bail, federal judges are not permitted to consider the danger to the community posed by a defendant in setting his bail. In fact, judges frequently carry on an informal, disguised practice of preventive detention by setting high bail when they want to detain dangerous defendants.

The difficulty of this issue is made painfully clear by a study conducted in the District of Columbia.[10] Analysis of arrest statistics suggests that approximately one-third of all crimes are committed by people on some form of non-custodial release—bail, personal recognizance, probation, or parole. The statistics also indicated that most people on noncustodial release do not commit crimes. (During the year-long study, only 10 percent of the people placed on noncustodial release were re-arrested.) Judges usually cannot tell in advance whether a particular defendant will be one of the many people who present no risk to the community or whether he is a threat.

The problems refuse to disappear; society must still grapple with how to design a bail system that meets its needs. Past reforms, such as the increased use of summonses in place of arrests, permitting a defendant to act as his own bondsman by posting a percentage of his bail with the court, and community supervison of people awaiting trial, should be applied more extensively. A greater use of guidelines that dictate pre-trial release practices would produce a more consistent, fairer release pattern. Ideally, the bail system should assure the community that dangerous defendants and those likely to flee before trial will be segregated and that all other defendants will be released on reasonable conditions, regardless of their wealth.

Those who cannot afford or who have been denied bail must await trial in jail; those who have been convicted and sentenced are usually housed in prisons. Over half a million people are housed in jails at some time during any one year. They include the innocent and the guilty, the truant youngster and the hired killer, the alimony dodger and the escaped felon. Although there was some jail reform during the 1970s, such reform has been almost exclusively a creation of the federal courts. While some prisons have amenities such as classrooms, exercise facilities, and craft shops, jails have very few or no

Jails

facilities for learning or even exercising because they are only "temporary" detention facilities.

The consequences of jail conditions frequently appear in reports of violence, riots, and suicide. A recent survey of 14 jails in one state suggested an explanation for this: nearly 80 percent of the inmates were awaiting trial; 70 percent were charged with minor offenses; and almost half were under 21 years of age.[11]

Most of the people in jail do not need to be detained, and many of those who need some kind of confinement should not be kept in jails. Juvenile status offenders—children who are truant or deemed beyond their parents' control—should not be housed with prostitutes, drunk drivers, and violent criminals. Efforts should also be made to empty the jails of those who simply need shelter or medical care, such as vagrants, the mentally disturbed, alcoholics, and addicts. Jails should be used to do only what they are designed to do—to detain dangerous people for short periods before trial.

During the coming decade, the federal government should assist local governments in developing new jail architecture, construction, and operation to ensure that, as institutions, jails serve their limited pre-trial detention function in a humane and productive manner. The correct long-term investments in jail reform will save society money in the long run. More importantly, a higher level of public safety is likely to result from reform than from the system of human warehousing now called jail.

The System and Its People: Trial Through Prison

Criminal courts and prisons are overburdened today and are likely to be subject to even greater demands in the next decade. The challenge facing the system, particularly the state courts, is how to manage this burgeoning workload sensibly and fairly.

Adjudication

The criminal court system, especially at the state level, today carries a workload too heavy for its resources. This is immediately apparent from the extensive use of plea bargaining, which now accounts for the disposition of more than 90 percent of all cases in state criminal courts. It is expected that the caseload of the state systems will continue to grow.

Approximately half the cases in the criminal courts arise between people who know each other fairly well; often there is a history of conflict between them. About 100 communities now offer mediation or arbitration services intended to help resolve such disputes outside of the courts. The results from these and other experimental non-judicial dispute resolution projects are encouraging; court caseloads drop in areas where such services are available.[12] The coordinated expansion of these programs should be considered carefully.*

Removing from the criminal courts those cases that could reasonably be settled elsewhere offers some relief for crowded dockets, but more will be needed. The present resources of the courts will have to be used more efficiently. For example, judicial training programs can be helpful, but they are rare; only Michigan and California offer statewide programs, and the two national organizations (the National Center for State Courts and the Judicial College) that have provided suitable training are presently without necessary federal financial support. The Panel endorses federal support of such projects.

Court management techniques should be studied and applied far more comprehensively than they have been. In particular, the National Center for State Courts should receive the support required to establish a program that would collect, analyze, and disseminate data about the changing circumstances and difficulties faced by state court systems. The circulation of such information would be of material benefit to agency planners, to the courts themselves, and ultimately to the public.

Sentencing: Capital Punishment, Prison, and Alternatives

The sentencing of convicted criminals is one of the most challenging responsibilities of the criminal justice system. The sentence given for a particular crime must reflect society's goals for the criminal justice system. Society has an interest in deterrence, rehabilitation, and the isolation of dangerous criminals. In pursuing these goals, judges must consider humaneness, fairness, and cost.

Some have proposed that judges be required to impose fixed sentences on defendants who have committed particular offenses, regardless of any mitigating factors. Under these mandatory sentencing laws, judges could not exercise any discretion in imposing sentences. A judge would have to give the same sentence to a hardened criminal as to a first offender, to a person with profound psychological problems as to a person who purposefully and knowingly committed the crime.

The Panel opposes mandatory sentencing laws. Although they may have greater deterrent effect than laws that allow judges some discretion, they can also produce great inequities in individual cases. Moreover, discretion cannot effectively be eliminated from the judicial system. If judges were deprived of their discretion in imposing

---

* The report of the Panel on the Electoral and Democratic Process discusses these programs in more detail.

114

sentences, they would find other, less public ways to exercise it.*

Capital punishment is the most controversial of sentencing options, though statistically the least significant. Clearly, it is not based on any notion of rehabilitation. There are less drastic, equally effective ways to preserve the security of society. Most studies of capital punishment suggest that it has little deterrent effect when compared to the prospect of a lifetime in prison. Further, blacks and other members of minority groups are more likely to receive a death sentence than whites with the same criminal record.

The Panel opposes capital punishment, not only because its imposition is inherently arbitrary and subject to abuse, but also because it offends the deepest sense of human rights. No matter how shocking murder, kidnapping, espionage, and other serious crimes may be, they do not justify the devaluation of human life represented by capital punishment.**

Imprisonment is the punishment imposed on slightly more than half of the people convicted of criminal offenses. Suspended sentences, probation, or fines are more frequently given to those who commit minor offenses. Those who commit serious crimes are almost always sentenced to prison.

Life in prisons is dangerous; homosexual rapes and violent assaults on inmates by their fellow prisoners occur every day. Although countless books and films document the viciousness of prison life, society confronts the horror of prison existence only rarely, such as when there is a prison riot. Despite numerous calls for reform, prisons remain dehumanizing institutions that have proved resistant to reform.

One source of the problem is overcrowding. Although the prison population showed a downward trend in the 1960s, this trend reversed in the 1970s. Rising prison populations resulted from a number of factors: more crimes and convictions, longer sentences, fewer paroles, and few new prison facilities. (Today, the cost of constructing new prisons is very high—approaching $40,000 per bed.)[13] In 1978, more than a quarter of a million people were incarcerated in federal or state prisons, almost all of

---

* For example, in Great Britain the repeal of the death penalty was followed by a sudden drop in the number of defendants who were found innocent by reason of insanity. The most logical explanation is that judges had acquitted defendants on that ground to avoid sending them to the gallows. *See* James Q. Wilson, *Thinking About Crime* (New York, 1975), p. 187.

** Commissioner Platten: Under some well-prescribed circumstances, the death penalty is appropriate. For that reason it should not be summarily abolished.

which were overcrowded. By 1979, more than half of the states had one or more prisons that were the subject of federal court orders and which were supervised by a U.S. District Court. Because of overcrowded prisons, sentenced offenders are often housed in jails, which themselves become overburdened.

One way of attacking the problem of brutality and overcrowding in prisons is through the use of alternative sentencing of convicted criminals. Models of alternative sentencing programs for convicted offenders already exist. Alternatives include the performance of services for the benefit of the community at large, intensive supervision in the community, restitution to the victims of crime, and the use of intermittent forms of confinement, including work release and day custody. These programs are more humane and can be considerably less expensive than imprisonment.

The Panel favors greater use of alternative sentences, but stresses that, in order to protect the community, some criminals must still be put in more secure institutions. The challenge for the next decade lies in expanding alternative sentencing programs and in making them subject to standards of rationality, fairness, and consistency.

A related issue for the 1980s is whether parole should be abolished. By 1974 most professional criminologists had concluded that prisons could not rehabilitate.[14] Therefore, some argue, indeterminate sentencing should no longer be permitted. These sentences permit parole boards to release prisoners who appear to have been rehabilitated before their full time is served. Instead, courts should impose, and prisoners serve, fixed sentences, and these sentences should be viewed as wholly punitive. This view is supported by the argument that parole decisions are highly subjective and therefore vulnerable to abuse.

The Panel cautions against hasty changes in public policy about parole. Instead, the Panel supports further research into the effects of different kinds of sentences on the criminal conduct of offenders. At present, the information is inadequate to support a conclusion favoring or rejecting coerced participation in rehabilitation programs, the abolition of parole, or increased harshness of sentences for particular offenses. Indeed, research done since 1974 has tended to contradict earlier findings.[15] In view of this uncertainty, the Panel stresses that in addition to rehabilitation and other goals, the basic principles of fairness and humaneness must govern every sentencing decision.

Juvenile Justice

The criminal justice system's approach to juvenile offenders has always been ambivalent.[16] Nominally, the goal of juvenile justice is to help youngsters, to prevent delinquents from becoming adult criminals. Yet, in practice, far more punishment than help is dispensed, an inevitable tendency in a system modeled on the system designed to punish adults who commit crimes.

The juvenile courts have become the dumping ground for many of society's problem children, a large number of whom present no threat to public safety. The courts handle cases involving juveniles who have committed a serious crime—armed robbery, assault, rape—but they also have authority over children who are neglected by their parents, who have committed minor crimes such as joyriding or shoplifting, or who are status offenders. In most jurisdictions status offenses include conduct classified as incorrigible or ungovernable, truancy, running away from home, and the like—acts that would not be criminal if the person were an adult.

In the past, these children were often put in closed institutions, locked up in training schools, juvenile detention facilities, and even adult jails. Due in large part to the leadership of the federal government in this field, far fewer status offenders and neglected children are now being imprisoned, but that form of punishment is still relatively common for youngsters who have committed minor property or more serious violent crimes.

The Panel supports the efforts of juvenile justice reformers around the country to remove as many children from locked institutions as possible and to remove all juveniles from adult jails and prisons. Like their adult counterparts, juvenile detention facilities can be cruel and inhumane environments.

Some have argued that the government should not be involved with neglected children or status offenders at all. The Panel disagrees. Society clearly has an obligation to intervene in many cases involving juveniles and to provide temporary shelter for children who suffer the effects of drug or alcohol abuse or who are the victims of abusive parents.

Others have proposed that jurisdiction over these children should be removed from the juvenile courts and given to a social welfare agency. Although juvenile judges are better trained to determine who has committed a crime than to deal with adolescent troubles, they are often more sensitive to the rights of the juvenile and his family than are social welfare agencies.

The most important issue in dealing with troubled juveniles who have not committed serious crimes is what kind of assistance they will receive, not who provides it. The Panel calls for greater support in local communities for counseling and treatment programs for neglected children and status offenders. Status offenses, particularly, should no longer be treated as pre-criminal behavior.

Although status offenders may be more likely than their peers to commit crimes as adults, in one study well over half of the children classed as status offenders did not grow up to be criminals.[17] The juvenile justice system has never been able to predict accurately which way a status offender will develop. Finally, the Panel supports the development and greater use of alternatives to full-time imprisonment for juveniles who have committed minor offenses and who pose little risk to the community. In particular, the Panel suggests that restitution to victims, supervised probation, compulsory community service, and periodic detention are alternatives that should be considered.

The handling of juveniles who commit serious, violent crimes (about 5 percent of juvenile court caseloads) is another troubling issue. Some propose treating older juveniles, those 16 and older, as adults—processing their cases in adult courts, imposing the harsher sentences normally given to adults, and housing juveniles in adult prisons.

Although a plausible case can be made for drawing the line between adults and juveniles at an age lower than 21, the Panel opposes the attempts to lower the age below 18. At 16 or 17 most adolescents lack many of the social ties—a job, family obligations, and financial commitments—that create pressures to conform to social norms. Not surprisingly, many juveniles who have been arrested "mature out" of a pattern of minor criminal conduct. Exposing juveniles to the adult criminal system would stigmatize them with an adult arrest or conviction record that might hinder their chances to conform successfully to social rules.

Racism and Criminal Justice

In recent years, major strides have been made toward reducing racism in the administration of criminal justice. For example, today there are significantly more minority police, lawyers, judges, and corrections officials than there were 10 years ago. Moreover, incidents of police brutality against minority citizens seem to have dropped in frequency.

Despite these improvements, discrimination still taints the criminal justice system. Many of the more obvious kinds of discrimination have been eliminated, but racism persists. For example, blacks receive an average sentence of 65 months for the federal offense of assault; whites, however, receive an average of 53 months for the same offense.[18] Some suggest that the disparity can be explained by differences in the prior conviction records of black and white defendants; others assert that the difference is due to biases against the poor and minority group members held by the predominantly white judiciary. Neither explanation accounts adequately for the disparities.

Equally important is the strong belief by most minorities that the criminal justice system is unfair to them. The results of public opinion surveys are startling. A Louis Harris poll in 1977 attempted to document the extent to which perceptions of discriminations differ across racial groups. Sixty-one percent of the blacks surveyed, and 23 percent of the whites, thought that blacks were discriminated against in the protection they were given against crime. Roughly 70 percent of the blacks surveyed, and less than 30 percent of the whites, thought that blacks were discriminated against in the way they were treated by police in general and if arrested for a crime.[19] These figures alone indicate a persistent and serious problem in the criminal justice system.

Improving the System

Equal justice under law is one of the most important goals of a democracy, and it is clear that many in the United States think this country has failed to meet it. The Panel strongly urges that every aspect of the criminal justice system be examined to detect and eliminate any remnant of racial or other types of discrimination.

The predicted crime rates in the 1980s will lead to strains on the traditional relationships between the local, state, and federal governments. Crime is usually a local problem, is best handled by a local system, but the fiscal resources of localities are unlikely to be adequate to counter the growing burden of criminal activity. Therefore, the state and the federal governments must use their resources to support local efforts.

The areas of concern highlighted by this report cover the entire criminal justice system, from victims' rights to the rights of the accused; from arrest, bail, and jail to prosecution and sentencing. All parts of the system are in need of substantial reform. Social justice in the 1980s cannot be attained without serious reforms in the criminal justice system.

1. U.S. Department of Justice, Law Enforcement Assistance Administration, National Criminal Justice Information and Statistics Service, *Sourcebook of Criminal Justice Statistics—1979,* eds. Timothy J. Flanagan, Michael J. Hindelang, and Michael R. Gottfredson (Washington, D.C., 1980), pp. 5, 25, 456, 600, 628, 630; U.S. Department of Justice, Federal Bureau of Investigation, *Uniform Crime Reports for the United States* (Washington, D.C., 1979).
2. *Uniform Crime Reports* (1968, 1977); American Bar Association, Section of Criminal Justice, Committee on Economic Offenses, *Final Report* (Washington, D.C., 1976); Michael C. Blumenthal, "American Graphic: Two Views of Crime and Criminals," *Washington Post,* 12 August 1980.
3. *Sourcebook,* pp. 170-171.
4. *Ibid.,* pp. 261, 336-337, 339, 467, 662, 821, 874.
5. *Ibid.,* pp. 462-463.
6. Charles Silberman, *Criminal Violence, Criminal Justice* (New York, 1978), pp. 348, 350.
7. *Sourcebook,* pp. 2, 4, 25, 39.
8. U.S. Department of Justice, Law Enforcement Assistance Administration, National Institute of Law Enforcement and Criminal Justice, National Criminal Justice Reference Service, *A Community Concern: Police Use of Deadly Force* (Washington, D.C., 1979), pp. 33, 70.
9. *Ibid.,* pp. 35, 89, 93.
10. District of Columbia Bail Agency, Statistical Analysis Center, J. Daniel Welsh and Deborah Viets, *The Pretrial Defender in the District of Columbia: A Report of the Characteristics and Processing of 1975 Defendants* (Washington, D.C., n.d.).
11. Ronald Goldfarb, *Jails: The Ultimate Ghetto of the Criminal Justice System* (Garden City, N.Y., 1975).
12. U.S. Department of Justice, National Institute of Justice, Roger F. Cook, Janice A. Roehl, and David I. Shepphard, *Neighborhood Justice Centers Field Test: Final Evaluation Report* (Washington, D.C., 1980), pp. 99-100.
13. *Jails: The Ultimate Ghetto.*
14. *Robert Martinson, "What Works?—Questions and Answers About Prison Reform," The Public Interest* 35 (Spring 1974).
15. J. Q. Wilson, "'What Works' Revisited: New Findings on Criminal Rehabilitation," *The Public Interest* 61 (Fall 1980): 3-17.
16. This discussion draws heavily on material presented by Silberman, *Criminal Violence,* pp. 418-501.
17. *Ibid.,* pp. 457-458.
18. National Minority Advisory Council on Criminal Justice, *The Inequality of Justice: A Report on Crime and the Administration of Justice in the Minority Community* (Washington, D.C., 1980).
19. Louis Harris, "The Harris Survey," *Chicago Tribune,* September 12, 1977, p. 3.

CONCLUDING
Statement

The recommendations in this report converge on four general themes. First, the country cannot put the matter of racial justice aside, or further delay its achievement. The federal government should strengthen the civil rights laws of the 1960s and 1970s to ensure that blacks, other minorities, and women continue to make progress toward equality. This theme is not confined to the recommendations in the chapter on civil rights. It applies as well to education, for the Panel believes that desegregated education is an essential element of quality education, and to criminal justice, where the Panel observes unequal treatment of white and blacks.

Second, the country should consolidate its many health and welfare programs—and to a lesser degree its education and criminal justice programs—into coordinated systems that accomplish overarching objectives. The Panel has made a special effort to define those objectives: a guaranteed minimum income that reaches the working poor and families with both parents present in the case of welfare, and care that is accessible and affordable for all in the case of health. During the 1980s the process of examining the individual programs to determine their value to the system must begin. This examination must not be conducted in a mean-spirited or punitive way. Rather, it should be a conscious effort to end the gaps between and the overlaps among the country's social programs.

Third, the country needs leadership that is responsive to social justice concerns. This leadership begins in the community, where much of the country's education and criminal justice policy is determined, and builds to the executive branch of the federal government, where major civil rights, health, and welfare decisions are made. The Panel has concluded its investigations convinced that progress in social justice is not solely a matter of social engineering; it requires leadership committed to making hard choices, outlining priorities, and working toward constructive change.

Fourth, the central concern expressed in this report is that the social justice needs of the nation be met. The fiscal

121

realities of the coming decade imply, however, that efficiency in the design and implementation of programs that address this objective will be an even more important consideration in the 1980s than in the past. As one of the Commissioners has expressed this idea, there are better and worse ways of spending any given level of money.

In the past, efficiency was considered to be a code word that meant the opposite of concern. Reaching social justice goals in this decade requires a synthesis that combines concern for people with a concern with spending public money wisely. It is the hope of the Panel that in civil rights, health, welfare, education, and criminal justice, this report will serve as a basis for just such a synthesis.

Additional
Views OF COMMISSIONER
BENJAMIN L. HOOKS

Statement on Education. I believe that in the 1980s our nation must rededicate itself to improving the quality and vitality of public education, despite the counsel of fiscal conservatives and others who urge that this is a time for political expediency and "practical" approaches to cutting back on society's commitment to academic excellence through the full and equal provisions of educational services.

Two and one-half years after the Supreme Court's 1954 decision in *Brown* v. *Board of Education,* our nation must not be sidetracked by the so-called efficacy of school desegregation, by the costs in terms of energy and other expenditures for public transportation, or by the "academic" needs of nonwhite students. Instead, we must assure all the nation's youth of an excellent education and equal educational opportunity so that they are trained to be productive contributors to our society.

I believe that there are serious deficiencies in the education report of the Panel. There can be no question that the themes of equity, competence, and excellence are good ones on which to base such an agenda; however, some attention must be given to how these goals are to be achieved. The report fails to do that. The education section of the report creates an impression that the shortcomings of our nation's schools stem from the demands of special interest groups, the breakdown of the communities where the schools are situated, confusion of purpose, and the proliferation of federal programs and regulations. I must take sharp issue with any implied or expressed statements or conclusions made in this regard.

Many of the problems of the schools, I believe, lie with the schools themselves. The major task of the 1980s must be restoring confidence and quality to the public schools. This requires a commitment to educate our nation's children. We must not focus on gimmicks or frills. We must ensure that schools fill their essential mission, which is to give students the basic skills and social experience required to be functional and productive citizens in a democratic society.

To achieve this goal, schools must be given the support of the community at large, and school personnel must be held accountable for the students' proficiency in acquiring and demonstrating the basic skills. Competence in reading, writing, ciphering, logical thinking, and fluency in the English language are basic to the requisite preparation of an individual to participate successfully in society. There competencies are the building blocks of an effective education.

I do not believe that some of the things called for in the education section of the report, such as a "a new spirit of collaboration" or "learning in community settings outside the schools" get to the root causes of the deteriorating quality of our public schools. Education is too important to our total society to dismiss with platitudes.

In the 1980s, if we are to have not just desegregated schools but racially integrated schools, there will have to be, in the first instance, a rethinking of the *Milliken* v. *Bradley* type prohibition of a city-suburban interdistrict remedy to segregated schools. The arbitrary, artificial school district lines that have been drawn between black districts and white districts must be recognized for what they are—barriers to equal educational opportunity and integrated schooling.

The federal government must continue to be involved in educational matters. Without a specific provision in the U.S. Constitution, even without a definitive statement from the U.S. Supreme Court as to whether education is a fundamental right of every citizen of the United States, I believe it is reasonable to conclude that in modern day society, education has been and should be accorded that status. By virtue of its increasing activity in the field of social and economic life, the federal government may be expected to act responsibly and often in expanding and equalizing educational opportunity.

Substantial questions relate to the federal government's role are tied to tax exemptions and private schools, tuition tax credit proposals, financial aid policies, affirmative action, desegregation, bilingualism, and the treatment of aliens, women, and legislatively protected groups. The flow of federal dollars in research, planning, and technology to specific educational institutions and the allocation of public monies and resources to the private sector in the training and development of scholars lead to no other conclusion than the reality of an ongoing and substantial federal involvement with education.

It is clear that there is still much to be accomplished if there is to be educational opportunity at all levels of education, and so the federal government should take the lead in pursuing remedies to both invidious discrimination and routine patterns of decisionmaking by local authorities that often contribute to (if not produce and structure) inequalities. For example, the financing of the public schools by a heavy reliance on local property tax revenues denies tangible equality to students in low-income school districts.

There is a further danger, I believe, that taxpayer revolts through popular referenda will interrupt sufficient levels of support for the public schools by compelling severe cutbacks in educational services. When this occurs, and as the cities become predominantly nonwhite and poor, the public schools will be increasingly dependent on the federal government for aid just to maintain otherwise costly educational progress. In this regard, public policy should not only support public education, it should discourage the flight of the middle class from the public schools. It is important, therefore, that the courts and Congress assist the Internal Revenue Service in denying tax exemptions to private white "segregation" academies on the ground that they are not set up primarily for educational purposes but to evade the law's desegregation mandate affecting the public schools. I also believe that the use of education vouchers will erode the public school system to the detriment of the millions of students who must depend on the public school system for an education.

I also feel that increased attention must be given to affirmative action in institutions of higher education in admissions and in hiring and promotional policies and practices. In addition, professional schools must be encouraged to act more responsibly and vigorously to open the fields of science, technology, business, and engineering to nonwhites and women and rapidly to increase their representation in medicine and law. In this regard, catalogues, textbooks, and instructional materials will have to be studied and revised to eliminate racial and sexual stereotyping, supplemented whenever necessary with in-service training and retraining of teaching and administrative staff.

I am not unaware of the economic crisis with which the nation is presently grappling and the cycle of inflation and retrenchment. However, I am also aware that as the society grows, its educational needs expand. The population, whether rising or declining, is in constant need of knowledge about science, technology, civics, economics, and human affairs. All the signs indicate that we are entering a period when we need the public schools most—to raise national literacy levels, to train people for new careers and developing industries, and to integrate minorities and new immigrants in the mainstream of American life.

Therefore, being fully cognizant of the national fixation regarding fiscal austerity, I am thoroughly convinced that unless our educational needs are given priority in terms of sufficient resource allocation, public support, administrative and Congressional initiatives to meet the mandates of *Brown* v. *Board of Education* and the macro-society, we will be mortgaging our future. Failure to address these problems through bold, concrete, comprehensive moral action will consign our children to a bleak and sorry life, unable to appreciate and unprepared to build upon the foundations of our democratic institutions.

Our children are virtually powerless to act for themselves. It is left to parents, citizens, public officials, and responsible leaders in communities across the nation to assume the role of advocates for educational efficiency and equality. The task is to raise the educational standards of long-neglected schools and to strengthen the system of public education.

Biographies

Dorothy I. Height is the National President of the National Council of Negro Women, Inc. Ms. Height received an M.A. degree from New York University. She has dedicated her career to the advancement of social justice. Ms. Height has been a leader of the civil rights movement and an active member of major national organizations for education, children and youth, religion, and human rights. She has received numerous honorary degrees and awards for her public service.

Dorothy I. Height

Benjamin L. Hooks is Executive Director of the National Association for the Advancement of Colored People (NAACP). Mr. Hooks was educated at LeMoyne College and Howard University and received a J.D. degree from DePaul University College of Law. He served as an Assistant Public Defender in Memphis and was the first black judge in Shelby County Criminal Court, Tennessee; he has also served as a Commissioner with the Federal Communications Commission. Mr. Hooks is a licensed minister affiliated with Baptist churches in Memphis and Detroit. He served on the board of the Southern Christian Leadership Conference and is a member of the American Bar Association and the Judicial Council of the National Bar Association.

Benjamin L. Hooks

Lane Kirkland is the President of the American Federation of Labor-Congress of Industrial Organizations (AFL-CIO). Mr. Kirkland is a graduate of the U.S. Merchant Marine Academy and Georgetown University. Prior to joining the AFL in 1948, he was a Licensed Master Mariner on merchant ships. He has held various union posts, including Director of Research and Education, International Union of Engineers, and Executive Assistant to the President and Secretary-Treasurer, AFL-CIO. Mr. Kirkland has served as a member of the U.S. Delegation to the International Labour Organization, the Commission on CIA Activities Within the United States, the National Commission on Productivity, and the Presidential Commission on Financial Structure and Regulation.

Lane Kirkland

Juanita M. Kreps is a former Secretary of Commerce. Ms. Kreps holds a Ph.D. in economics and has served as Vice President of Duke University. She has been a teacher and an administrator, the author of several books and many articles in economic journals, and a member of state and federal advisory councils. Ms. Kreps presently is a member of the boards of R. J. Reynolds Industries, J. C. Penney Co., Citicorp, Eastman Kodak, and American Telephone and Telegraph, and is a trustee of the Duke Endowment.

Juanita M. Kreps

Esther Landa is a member of the President's Advisory Committee for Women; she chairs the subcommittee on education. Ms. Landa holds the B.A. and M.A. degrees from Mills College. She is active in national volunteer organizations, including the League of Women Voters, Head Start, and the United Fund. Ms. Landa served as President of the National Council of Jewish Women and was presiding officer at the National Women's Conference in Houston in 1977. In July 1980, she served as a member of the United States delegation to the United Nations Mid-Decade Conference for Women.

Esther Landa

Martin E. Marty is the Fairfax M. Cone Distinguished Service Professor at The University of Chicago, where he earned his Ph.D. Mr. Marty is Associate Editor of *The Christian Century,* Editor of the newsletter *Context,* and Co-Editor of *Church History.* His numerous books include *Righteous Empire,* for which he won the National Book Award. Mr. Marty is a former President of the American Society of Church History, and is currently President of the American Catholic Historical Association.

Martin E. Marty

Donald C. Platten is Chairman and Director of the Chemical New York Corporation and the Chemical Bank. Mr. Platten joined the Chemical Bank after his graduation from Princeton University in 1940. He is also a Director of the Associated Dry Goods Corporation, CPC International, Inc., the New York Chamber of Commerce and Industry, the United Way of New York City, the Association of Reserve City Bankers, the Economic Development Council of New York City, Inc., and the National Minority Purchasing Council. He is a member of the Federal Advisory Council of the Federal Reserve System and the Council on Foreign Relations. Mr. Platten is Chairman of the New York City Mayor's Management Advisory Committee and of Goodwill Industries of Greater New York, Inc.

Donald C. Platten

Tomás Rivera is Chancellor at the University of California at Riverside. Mr. Rivera received his M.Ed. from Southwest Texas State University and his Ph.D. from the University of Oklahoma. He has served as Executive Vice President of The University of Texas at El Paso and as Vice President for Administration for The University of Texas at San Antonio. Mr. Rivera is a member of the board of trustees for the Carnegie Foundation for the Advancement of Teaching and of the executive committee of the National Council of Chicanos in Higher Education. He is a writer and poet, and a recipient of the *Premio Quinto Sol,* National Literary Award.

Tomás Rivera

Leon B. Schachter is a former Vice President and Regional Director of the United Food and Commercial Workers International Union, AFL-CIO & CLC, and a former President of the Amalgamated Food & Allied Workers Union, Local 56, in New Jersey. Mr. Schachter has been active in union affairs nationally and internationally for many years, in 1940 negotiating the first labor-management contract with a U.S. corporate farm. He has also served on several national advisory groups and participated in the White House Conferences on Food and Nutrition and on Aging.

Leon B. Schachter

Lewis Thomas is Chancellor of the Memorial Sloan-Kettering Cancer Center. Dr. Thomas was educated at Princeton University and received his M.D. from Harvard Medical School. His many academic appointments include Chairman, Department of Medicine, New York University-Bellevue Medical Center; Dean, New York University School of Medicine; and Dean, Yale University School of Medicine. Dr. Thomas has been an active member on many state and federal public health and science advisory committees. He received the National Book Award in Arts and Letters for *The Lives of a Cell,* and the Christopher Award for *The Medusa and the Snail.*

Lewis Thomas

Addie L. Wyatt is International Vice President and Direc tor, Civil Rights and Women's Affairs Department, United Food and Commercial Workers International Union, AFL-CIO & CLC. Ms. Wyatt is also Executive Vice President of the Coalition of Labor Union Women and a member of the National Commission on Working Women and the Coalition of Black Trade Unionists. She is active in community affairs in Chicago, where she serves as a labor adviser to the Chicago Urban League, to Roosevelt University, and to Operation PUSH (People United to Save Humanity). She is especially concerned with child care issues.

Addie L. Wyatt

129

Edward D. Berkowitz, a member of the Senior Professional Staff of the Panel on Government and the Advancement of Social Justice, is the author of several books and articles on social welfare history, including the recently published *Creating the Welfare State.* Mr. Berkowitz, a graduate of Princeton University, holds a Ph.D. in American history from Northwestern University. He has taught at Northwestern and at the University of Massachusetts at Boston.

Edward D. Berkowitz

Raymond F. Reisler, a member of the Senior Professional Staff of the Panel on Government and the Advancement of Social Justice, has served as a Special Assistant in the Office of the U.S. Commissioner of Education. Mr. Reisler received a B.S. from Cornell University and a Ed.D. from the University of Massachusetts at Amherst. He has served as a VISTA volunteer and a public school teacher and principal, and has taught at the University of Calgary, Canada.

Raymond F. Reisler

Stuart O. Schweitzer, a member of the Senior Professional Staff of the Panel on Government and the Advancement of Social Justice, is Head of the Division of Health Services of the School of Public Health at the University of California at Los Angeles. Mr. Schweitzer received his Ph.D. in economics from the University of California. He has taught economics at Wayne State University and Georgetown University and has held research appointments at the Urban Institute and the National Institutes of Health.

Stuart O. Schweitzer

Index